If
Success
is a Game,
These
are the
Rules

ALSO BY CHÉRIE CARTER-SCOTT, PH.D.

If Love is a Game, These are the Rules: Ten Rules for Finding Love and Creating Long-Lasting, Authentic Relationships

If Life is a Game, These are the Rules: Ten Rules for Being Human

Negaholics: How to Overcome Negativity and Turn Your Life Around

The Corporate Negaholic: How to Deal Successfully with Negative Colleagues, Managers, and Corporations

The New Species: The Evolution of the Human Being

The Inner View: A Woman's Daily Journal

Chicken Soup for the Global Soul, coauthored with Jack Canfield and Mark Victor Hansen, scheduled to be published in summer 2001

CHÉRIE CARTER-SCOTT, PH.D.

IF SUCCESS IS A GAME, THESE ARE THE RULES

*Ten Rules for a
Fulfilling Life*

Broadway Books   New York

BROADWAY

Library of Congress Cataloging-in-Publication Data
Carter-Scott, Chérie.
If success is a game, these are the rules: ten rules for a fulfilling life / Chérie Carter-Scott.—1st ed.
p. cm.
1. Success—Psychological aspects. I. Title.
BF637.S8 C378 2000
158.1—dc21   99-049320

FIRST EDITION

ISBN 0-7679-0426-5

00 01 02 03 04 10 9 8 7 6 5 4 3 2 1

I dedicate this book to my father, Milton F. Untermeyer, who taught me about success through his attitude, actions, and behaviors. His example inspired me to never give up in the pursuit of all my dreams.

I also dedicate this book to my mentor and friend, Warren Bennis, who believed in me and has been my role model in my professional life.

ACKNOWLEDGMENTS

Debra Goldstein, my alter ego, who helps me articulate, define, recall, clarify, and listen to the guidance that wants to be captured in this book.

Lauren Marino, my editor, believes in merging spiritual principles with daily experience. Her guidance, direction, and feedback ensure that this book will put people on the path to success in everything they are looking for.

Bob Barnett and Jackie Davies, my guardian angels for whom I am dearly grateful.

Stephen Rubin believes in me, my vision, experience, and the wisdom of the *Game—Rules* books.

Donna Gould, my publicist, is dedicated, committed, and indefatigable in her mission.

Linda Michaels, who is committed to the entire world knowing this message.

Pat Brozowski, Bob Burt, Joe Netherland, Jeff Garnes, Jeff Jacoby, Jim Bell, Judy Smeltzer, Rob Christie, Bill Granville, Jim Veny, Rita Butler, Jim and Barbara Ballard, Cathy Swigon, Jeff Link, Tom Kline, and all the folks at FMC, who are willing to go through the exciting yet uncomfortable process of continuing success at higher levels.

Robert Allen ensures that the books are available. Debbie Stier masterminds all publicity efforts.

Lynn Stewart, my sister and business partner for twenty-five years, is the "wind beneath my wings." Her support is unsurpassed.

Rachel Goldberg, who attends to whatever is needed and wanted with the spirit of an angel.

Sara Nelson, enthusiastic and dedicated to having the greatest number of people have satisfaction and fulfillment in their lives.

Judy Rossiter, who is the main contact for people who want to experience their power.

Michael Pomije, my beloved, my soul mate and my partner, who supports me in my visions, dreams, and goals.

To all those individuals and organizations who have allowed the MMS Institute, Inc., to empower them on their path. It is from these experiences that this book is written.

CONTENTS

Contents

Contents

Rule Nine : Every Level of Success Brings New Challenges. 196

EACH ACCOMPLISHMENT ALTERS YOUR REALITY, EITHER SLIGHTLY OR

DRAMATICALLY. YOUR TASK IS TO MAINTAIN YOUR BALANCE WHEN

YOUR GAME BOARD SHIFTS.

Rule Ten : Success Is a Process That Never Ends. 223

EACH PLATEAU HAS A NEW ASCENT. ONCE YOU REACH THE TOP,

THERE IS YET A NEW PEAK TO EMBRACE.

If one advances confidently in the direction of his dream
and endeavors to live the life which he has imagined,
he will meet with a success unexpected in common hours.
If you have built castles in the air, your work need not be lost;
that is where they should be.
Now put foundations under them.

—Henry David Thoreau

INTRODUCTION

When I first started to explore the "Rules for Success," I felt that I must first define what I mean by "success." I thought long and hard about the word "success." I interviewed people I knew and approached many I didn't know to get a sense of what success means to them. I then researched biographies of famous people who had lived what appear to be successful lives, and it was then that the first truth emerged: Success means different things to different people.

I probed a bit deeper and found that underneath each person's vision, dreams, and goals nestled one essential core: a universal desire for fulfillment. Even though some may dream of riches, others of fame, and still others of making a difference, all of them agree that to be fulfilled was the ultimate measurement of success. Even Warren Buffett, one of the wealthiest men in the world, pinpointed happiness as the key defining element of true success.

The next appropriate question I felt compelled to ask was: What is the difference between success and fulfillment? I discovered that success is measured primarily by standards outside ourselves, while fulfillment is assessed internally. No one can deem you fulfilled except you. However, the world, with its objective criteria, can and does judge you as successful if you measure up to its standards.

If the world judges you as successful, it means either that you have realized your own goals and expectations or that you may have exceeded normal, average standards held by the majority of people. Accomplishments are the main barometer the world uses to measure success: breaking records, amassing fortunes, being the first to do something, or changing current mind-sets all qualify. Being the best at something, conquering, curing, breaking through some barrier all deem one eligible to enter the hallowed halls of success.

Fulfillment, however, is something quite different. Fulfillment is a feeling that comes from within your soul that radiates through your being. It is the feeling of deep satisfaction and contentment you experience at the end of the day when you lie in bed before drifting off into sleep, knowing in your heart and your bones that you have met or exceeded your expectations of yourself. To be fulfilled means to be "filled full" with a sense of well-being.

When your own sense of well-being and the external symbols of accomplishment converge, then you have achieved "success." One without the other is like a candle without a match: Each can exist separately, but when used together, the resulting flame creates a miraculous glow.

The following rules for a fulfilling life are not the steps to the magic kingdom of prosperity. Rather, these rules are the universal truths that underlie all successful endeavors and individuals. They are the essence of what connects us as human beings who desire to realize our potential.

If you desire success, then you must walk the path of those who have previously left their footprints in the sand. Tracing their steps, you find your own essential truth so that you may leave your own prints, which define your own personal experience of success.

To know the essence of success, you will need to travel through these universal truths. Even if I had not laid them before you here, chances are you would have encountered them along your way. The purpose of this book is to expedite your learning and facilitate your personal journey toward a fulfilling life.

May you uncover your own definition of success and tread fruitfully down the path toward its realization. I wish for you the discovery of your inner truths, the conviction to believe in yourself, the wherewithal to find your way, and the courage to rise when the world expects you to fall. May you learn the lessons life places before you and accomplish all that will provide you with deep, authentic fulfillment and happiness.

Enjoy the journey.

Blessings,
Chérie Carter-Scott, Ph.D.

IF
SUCCESS
IS A GAME,
THESE
ARE THE
RULES

RULE ONE

Each Person Has Their Own Definition of Success

There is no universal definition of "success." Everyone has their individual vision of what it means to be fulfilled.

Success is many things. It is both a concept and an experience, a moment as well as an evolution. It is the merging of your aspirations with reality, the weaving of your hopes and dreams with your daily tasks. It is simultaneously tangible and ephemeral, and gives the illusion of being universally quantifiable. Success is externally evaluated yet intrinsically experienced; it is both objective and subjective. The true essence of success, beneath the visible markers and goals, lies in your own personal sense of satisfaction and fulfillment.

What comes to mind for you when you think about "success"?

What are the images you see? What does it feel like in your bones to have succeeded? Do you imagine reaching the apex of your profession? Or do you imagine amassing great wealth? Does it mean seeing your face on the cover of national magazines or reading your name in *Who's Who*?

For some people success may be any one or all of these. For others it may be something entirely different, such as earning enough money to retire at fifty, or having their own art show in a gallery, or coaching their child's little league team to victory. To some success looks like grand achievement, to others it resembles daily rewards, and still others measure it as the accomplishment of an underlying life mission. It may mean being a good friend, or raising socially responsible children, or being a loving grandparent. For some the achievement looks like having lived ethically, honorably, or according to their values and conscience. For many finding or sustaining a romantic relationship or marriage is a goal. Overcoming a disability, hardship, challenge, or obstacle is the criteria for some, whereas breaking records—athletic, financial, historic, or scientific—is where fulfillment lies for others.

Since each person is an individual, comprised of his or her own visions and standards, each person defines success in his or her own way. My definition is probably not the same as yours, nor is yours exactly the same as that of other people you know. We are a constellation of individuals, each holding our own place in the cosmos and twinkling from within as a result of whatever gives us our own individual glow. The first basic rule of success, and perhaps the most important, is that there is no one universal definition of fulfillment. We each have our own, and every one is equally precious and worthy.

THE STANDARDS OF SUCCESS

The popular cultural definition of success in industrial nations is based primarily on three elements: power, money, and fame. It is assumed that if you are in possession of great abundance, have status or power, or are recognized as a celebrity, then you are, by society's definition, "successful." If you have even one of those three requirements, you qualify.

There is, however, one major problem with this definition: It is severely limited. It excludes a multitude of people who are successful in their own right and who define success by an entirely different set of standards. These are the people whose bank balances may not be especially noteworthy, who do not brandish significant authority, and who are not necessarily recognized when they walk down the street. Rather, these are the people who have realized goals and dreams that have been set from within rather than those dictated by societal norms.

Consider the school principal who started a middle school that teaches children values, self-esteem, and love of nature. Is creating an environment where children grow in healthy ways and develop awareness and values any less successful than the business tycoon who masterminds corporate buyouts?

Consider the person who volunteers at a local hospital to read to the elderly whose eyes can no longer perform the task.

Is this person any less of a success than the professional ballplayer who scores the winning run as the most valuable player?

Think about the scientist who has dedicated her life to finding a cure for cancer. Is she considered a success only if she actually finds the cure? Do the hours and dedication she has put forth count only if the result is achieved? Is success measured only in the culmination, or is the commitment, the perseverance, and the pursuit valued as well?

What about the middle-age man who leaves his law practice to pursue his dream of carving and selling canoes? If his delight is in doing what makes him happy, is he any less prosperous than the celebrity who grosses $10 million per movie?

Success is amorphous, and like the other vast intangible—love—there is no universal means by which we can measure it. What it means for one person may not resonate for another. It may be the collective goal of many, but it ultimately has only one true judge. You, and only you, can assess your success, for it is you alone who determines what success really means for you.

THE DIFFERENT MODELS OF SUCCESS

Make sure you have—and preserve—your own set of eyes.
— LAURIE BETH JONES

Dana was in her thirties when she came to my workshop because she was experiencing what she called a "free-floating sense of dissatisfaction" with her job. She enjoyed the high-level position she held at a large computer company, but a small voice in her heart whispered to her that there was more. She had achieved each and every goal she had set before her, including promotions, raises, and even a much-coveted window office, yet she was not fulfilled.

As Dana talked, I picked up on phrases like "I should feel happy" and "I look successful but I feel like a failure." So I asked Dana point blank what would make her feel like a success. She paused for less than fifteen seconds before blurting out "being able to bring my dog to work."

It seems that Dana had always had a vision in her mind of being able to bring her beloved dog, Bodhi, with her to work. She had once visited a friend at her friend's small boutique advertising agency and was delighted to see the agency owner's schnauzer greeting clients at the door. To Dana, being able to bring her dog to work signified autonomy; it meant one of two things: Either she had climbed high enough on the corporate ladder that she was beyond policies, or she was running her own company where she could establish her own rules. Deciding between the two was not difficult for her, and Dana is now happily running her own web design business, with Bodhi snoozing contentedly under her desk.

For some people, like Dana, success is synonymous with autonomy. For others it looks like financial freedom. Troy, for example, had a desire to earn enough money so that he could retire at age fifty and spend his days traveling around the world with his wife. To him, success meant being able to afford to do the things he wanted to do and to enjoy himself.

To Jeff, a stock broker in his forties, success was also

measurable in financial terms. His, however, were different from Troy's. His vision was to be able to make enough money to buy a home for his aging parents in Las Vegas for their retirement. Jeff was enormously grateful to his parents for all they had done for him, including both of them working two jobs to put him through college. Taking care of them in their later years would be Jeff's ultimate joy and satisfaction.

Nina, an interior decorator who traveled extensively, did not relish dealing with logistics. When she dreamed of prosperity, it was with the vision of being able to hire people to help her with things like repairing her computer when it crashed, installing shelves in her closets, cleaning her apartment when she couldn't find the time, arranging her travel plans, and so on. To Nina, fulfillment came in the form of making enough money to hire people to support her with her busy life.

For some people success is defined as emotional fulfillment and stability. Sondra's childhood was difficult and tumultuous, and she set a goal to create a happy, harmonious home for her family. Every night, when she sits down to dinner with her husband and three children, she is flooded with a sense of fulfillment. To Sondra, success is achieved each moment she experiences the joy of being together with her family.

Many—dare I hope most?—parents deem raising their children well as a sign of success. Although Jacqueline Kennedy Onassis was an internationally known personality who enjoyed a prosperous lifestyle and had many glamorous and exciting experiences, she held her job as a parent as singularly most important. "If you bungle raising your kids," she is quoted as saying, "I don't think whatever else you do well matters very much."

Success can be defined as glory, as it is for the athlete who wins a race or a mountain climber who scales Mount Everest. Those in the armed services who serve their country might define success in these terms as well.

Courage can be the model for success, as it is for those who must reach inside themselves for the stamina to overcome a serious illness or those who must face tragedies in life. Helen Keller is perhaps the most famous name symbolizing courage, as her triumph in life from within her sightless, soundless world stands as a symbol of what the human spirit is capable of. Her legacy includes one of my favorite quotes: "Life is either a daring adventure, or nothing." Helen Keller's life was certainly the former.

Another definition of success is making a difference. One way to make a difference is to change the way people perceive reality. Elisabeth Kübler-Ross was the first person to publicly confront the concept of grief within the medical community, and as a result, the world came to understand and embrace a completely new way of dealing with loss. Her lifelong efforts put the heart back into the practice of medicine. To her, and to others like her, success meant changing the status quo.

Perhaps the accumulation of knowledge and understanding is what spells success for you. Leonardo da Vinci was fascinated by the nature of man and his place in the universe. Days before his death, Leonardo wrote: "As a well-spent day brings happy sleep, so does a well-used life bring happy death." Although his life ended in relative poverty and obscurity, it is clear from his words that he viewed his time here as a success. It was success based on his terms of a fruitful life spent seeking the truth in all things—philosophy, art, music, anatomy, mathematics—and then sharing it with others.

For me, having a profound impact on one person's life means that my life was not lived in vain. Each time I lead a workshop and see the spark ignite in one participant's eye, I feel as if I have succeeded. Seeing people change their behaviors, fulfilling their dreams, ending a cycle of self-sabotage, beginning to earnestly love themselves is what brings me a deep sense of fulfillment.

Clearly, no one definition of success is better than another. Desiring financial abundance is no less worthy than aspiring to have your face on the cover of a magazine or aiming to get a bill passed in Congress. Mother Teresa's goal of aiding the poor and hungry is certainly noble but is no less valid than that of Richard, one of my clients, who aspired to own and operate his own pastry shop.

Whether your dream is dollars or satisfaction, sainthood or popularity, fame or authenticity, what makes your dream worthy and real is that it is yours. You alone set the standard of what it means for you to succeed in life, for it is you alone who knows what will truly fulfill you in your heart and make your life worth living.

Your Personal Definition of Success

Insist on yourself. Never imitate.

—Ralph Waldo Emerson

What does success mean to you? What will it take for you to feel fulfilled in life? To what do you aspire?

Establishing your personal definition of success is important because it will prevent you from spending precious time and energy pursuing goals that hold no true luster for you. It can be easy to follow the status quo and aim for the usual markers. Despite the fact that the world may applaud such efforts, however, goals that you are not authentically connected to are essentially meaningless.

With the achievement of every inauthentic goal, most likely you will feel a sense of emptiness rather than a sense of satisfaction, since miscellaneous goals carry you farther from your ultimate fulfillment. If you follow cultural expectations blindly and pursue wealth, power, or fame simply because you think that is what you are supposed to want, then grabbing these brass rings will feel meaningless. If you lack the connection to your own personal values, then you may wake up one day having achieved your goals but feeling disconnected from yourself.

If you reach for the corner office but do not truly aspire to it, the views will never really leave you breathless. If you know that success for you means building a cabin in the woods and living Thoreau's life of peaceful solitude, then each public accolade of your latest public relations coup will ring hollow in your ears. If you amass a fortune but privately measure prosperity according to different standards, the money in the bank will never meet your deepest needs. A dream realized that is not your own dream is like being served a scrumptious ice cream sundae made with flavors you don't really like. It looks enticing, but the taste does not satisfy your true preferences.

Knowing What Success Means to You

You can begin to know what success means to you only by first taking apart the cultural dictates that you may have been living by and examining them to determine if they ring true for you. Importance, clout, VIP status, luxury cars, affluent addresses, a "normal" marriage, and expensive watches are external measurements of what our society generally views as the symbols of success. Perhaps that is because these are the markers that are the most universally appealing to many people. If these elements beckon to you, then you can weave your vision of success from them. You can pursue your dream and work toward earning or attaining the rewards that bring you joy.

Often, however, people pursue the popular trappings and/or goals without really knowing why. Perhaps they become caught up in the treadmill of "keeping up with the Joneses." When success is pursued as proof of your worthiness, you are giving your life and your efforts over to the assessment of others. On the other hand, when success is pursued as the alignment of your innermost values and your goals become the validation of your inner truth, you honor your presence here on Earth as meaningful and authentic.

Success can be assessed externally by observers evaluating whether you have met a standard established by society; however, at the end of the day, there is either a peaceful feeling within you or there is emptiness. The peaceful feeling signals that you have lived up to your expectations and personal visions for yourself. The emptiness is a clue that you were striving toward a definition of success and fulfillment that was never really yours to begin with.

Establishing Your Vision

To help my clients formulate their visions, I give them the following exercise, which almost always excavates what it is that brings them fulfillment:

Complete the following sentences by writing down your responses on a blank sheet of paper. It is not sufficient merely to complete the sentences in your mind as you read them; you must commit your answers to paper. You can change what you wrote after you see them in print, but make sure you write them down.

1. The people I view as successful are . . .
2. I feel successful when I . . .
3. My symbols of success are . . .
4. I will feel like a success when I . . .
5. If I were to write my ideal obituary based on the fact that my life was a success, it would read like this . . .

For example, as a response to the first statement, you might list those people whom you know personally who appear successful to you, like the president of your company, a member of your club, or Bob your neighbor, who just installed a swimming pool in his backyard. Or you might list people you don't know personally but admire from afar, such as an accomplished athlete, a business mogul, or a respected journalist. By identifying your role models, you can see whom you admire and then specify what attributes and behaviors you choose to emulate.

For example, Bianca listed her deceased grandmother, Rose, as someone she admired for fulfilling her goal. Rose was a remarkably intelligent and feisty woman, and although it was almost unheard of in her day for women to go to college, she fought to be allowed to attend the university in the city close to her home. Despite the strong objections of her family, the disapproval of her small town, and the numerous obstacles placed in her path by the admissions board, Rose attended the university and earned a degree in medicine. Rose then went on to become a surgeon at a time when women were still mandated to cover their ankles and expected to stay at home and behave in a ladylike fashion.

Upon further reflection, Bianca saw that it was Rose's courage in the face of adversity that she was drawn to, and realized that this was a quality she wanted to possess within herself. When she was diagnosed with throat cancer several years later, long after Rose had passed away, Bianca called upon her spiritual connection to her grandmother to help her find the inner strength to overcome her illness.

To answer the second statement, "I feel successful when I . . ." think of the moments in life when you have felt truly fulfilled. Is it when you have achieved something? When you have received praise or validation from others? When you have had an impact on others' lives? <u>What is it that gives you the feeling that you are fulfilling your potential?</u> Knowing this answer will show you the way toward the path that is most likely to spell success for you.

In response to the second statement, Abe, a car salesman, wrote: "I feel successful when I see my commission check exceeding X dollars each month." For Abe, reaching a specific monetary goal boosted his confidence in his sales ability and enabled him to feel successful in his accomplishment.

The completion of the third statement, "My <u>symbols of success are</u> . . ." will enable you to see what <u>tangible results</u> you want to manifest in life. The symbols of success can be anything from a significant bank balance, to an abundance of free time, to fitting into a size-ten dress. Be as specific as you can, since your answers will provide clues to the lifestyle that conforms to your overall personal vision of success.

Completing the fourth statement, "<u>I will feel like a success when I</u> . . ." gives you the chance to try on your future aspirations to see how they will feel. There is something very powerful about putting "I" in front of all your desires. For example, remember Dana with her dog. It was one thing for her to say that her definition of success was being able to bring her dog to work. However, by clearly stating "I will feel successful when I am able to bring my dog to work," she placed herself into her vision. Putting "I" into the statement put her in the picture and gave her ownership over her wish.

Last, while the fifth question, "<u>If I were to write my ideal obituary based on the fact that my life was a success, it would read like this</u> . . ." might seem gloomy, it is actually one of the most instrumental and inspiring exercises you can do. Gary

Wollin, my personal financial planner, a brilliant man whose life is dedicated to supporting people's financial goals, asked me to complete this exercise. He finds that when people truly know what they want their lives to be about, then they can have their finances support their intentions.

I notice that many people put off doing this exercise because it confronts them with the reality of their mortality. I have found, conversely, that when you really examine your life head-on, you can be painfully honest about what you want to accomplish throughout your life. It is a bit uncomfortable writing down big dreams because they may sound highly ambitious or self-aggrandized, but unless you allow yourself to imagine your ideal life, you can never begin to make it happen. Imagining yourself at the end of your life looking back is a helpful tool to articulate what it is that you hope to accomplish during your lifetime.

Find a comfortable, quiet place where you can focus without distractions. Begin by writing or typing your life story as it reads up to this moment. Write it in the past tense and in third person. For example, "He was born in . . ." and so on. Include all the relevant moments, accomplishments, events, and experiences that have contributed to your development up until now.

The second part should begin as of tomorrow and move forward from that point until the day you die. This, too, should be written in the past tense, since it is, after all, your obituary. Write it as if all your dreams came true, and you fulfilled all of your heart's desires. Make this obituary the most meaningful, powerful expression of your fulfilled life. Include anything and everything that you can imagine yourself doing, and include some items that you cannot quite envision but might like to in a perfect world. Here is the place to break out of the oh, I-could-never trap and allow your imagination and ambitions to run wild.

While you are writing, don't edit or judge what you write. Rather, put every wish, hope, dream, goal, or aspiration down on paper as they come to you. Later you can edit what you wrote if you choose. After you are finished, look closely at what you said you did with your life and ask yourself if this is what you would like to become the reality. If it isn't, revise your obituary as you like. (That's the beauty of writing it while you are still alive!) When you are satisfied with it, put it in a place where you can reread it on a regular basis and begin to strategize how you will make it come true.

The most defining description there is about success is that it cannot be universally interpreted. Each person has his or her own vision of what it means to succeed and what it means to be successful, which is every bit as personal and unique as a thumbprint. The secret to achieving your own success is to search your heart for what matters to you and to set the standard of what you aspire to. Armed with that knowledge, your chances of succeeding at or in whatever you desire multiply a thousandfold. You can take the courageous leap onto your path and begin the journey toward personal fulfillment and, ultimately, the satisfying life you deserve.

RULE TWO

Wanting Success Is the First Step Toward Attaining It

*When you experience the initial spark of desire,
you set the game of success in motion.*

S uccess is a process that begins from within. It starts as a glimmer of hope, then evolves into a thought that plants a seed of promise inside your soul. It is a journey whose initial step is paved with an inner stirring. Whatever your dream may be, the dream needs to be activated into a desire before you can make it happen. In other words, first you need to actively want success if you ever hope to attain it.

This rule of success is so basic that you might be wondering why it is necessary to point out at all. After all, who among us does not want to succeed in life? Is there anyone who needs to stop and ask if they would rather be at the top of their game, enjoying the fruits of their efforts, as opposed to the middle of the pack or the bottom of the heap?

Ask yourself this: If everyone wanted to succeed, why isn't everyone successful? The answer is because not everyone fully grasps the fact that success is attainable only to those who possess the courage and conviction to say "I want it."

Let's imagine you have a fascination with boats. Whenever you drive past the ocean or eat at a restaurant by a marina, you think about how much fun it would be to own a boat. You might even fantasize about what kind of a boat it would be— a catamaran, a powerful speedboat, or a luxury yacht—and you can imagine the fun times you would have on the water, cruising around crystal-blue waters and breathing in the fresh salty air. Perhaps you wistfully remark to your spouse or friends from time to time that it would be nice to own a boat.

Given this scenario, it is not likely that you will become the owner of a boat any time in the near future, unless one mysteriously floats your way. Why? Because "It would be nice" is not the same as "I want it." It just doesn't carry the same intensity, drive, or causality.

"It would be nice" is a passive, somewhat vague wish, whereas "I want it" gives you ownership of your desire and puts you in the picture. "It would be nice" externalizes your desire and distances you from it; "I want it" brings it within your reach. Concrete, substantiated desire puts you in the driver's seat, whereas vague wishes keep you imprisoned in your own backseat. Owning your desire is the key that starts the engine of success.

It all starts with wanting. Wanting something different

from your current circumstances is the moment of engagement. Identifying the changes you want to make initiates the momentum and sets the process of success in motion. You may not always get what you want, but you can be certain that you will never attain your objectives if you don't begin with that initial seedling called "wanting."

THE POWER OF WANTING

Nothing in this world is impossible to a willing heart.

—ABRAHAM LINCOLN

No Super Bowl team in the history of football ever won the Vince Lombardi trophy out of musing "It would be nice if. . . ." Team members wanted to win, probably so deeply and fiercely that they would have moved Heaven and Earth to make it happen. It was that intense desire that fueled their determination, which in turn propelled them to success.

It is the same for individuals. When you want something— really want it—there is an internal reaction that goes off inside you that says "*yes*." That impulse is as strong when you are five years old reaching for a toy as it is when you are fifty reaching for your dream home. The energy that is unleashed in that moment of desire creates one of the most powerful and magnetic forces in the universe.

When I was twenty-one years old, my then-husband and I knew we wanted to backpack around the Hawaiian Islands after graduation. We both deeply wanted to take this trip, to explore the raw and astonishing wonders of Hawaii that no tour bus could ever reach. We wanted to give ourselves the chance to live off only that which we could carry on our backs, to connect with the greater world of nature. Real life was imminently upon us, and we wanted to pause and take a moment to have an experience like this before turning our attention to careers and the business of building a life.

I wanted this adventure so much that I would have done almost anything to make it happen. Despite limited funds and the disdain and protests of some family members, Bill and I strapped on our backpacks and went. The three months we spent exploring hidden caves, meeting indigenous people, and learning about the ancient customs, eating fruit we picked with our own hands, and swimming in secluded grottoes remain one of my most precious memories. The success of making that trip a reality was among the sweetest I have ever known. I doubt, however, that it would have happened if we had operated from a sense of "It would be nice to backpack in the Hawaiian Islands, wouldn't it?"

Think of a moment sometime in your life that you knew with every fiber of your being that you wanted something. It could be a particular trip, or a specific relationship, or even a piece of your grandmother's famous cheesecake. Would you have moved the heavens to attain your wish?

Wanting is a deep desire that emanates from within you. It defies reason, logic, and rational thought. It is an undeniable feeling, a flash of how things might be. Whether the impulse is to redecorate your bathroom, take a trip, or close a deal, "wants" are moments of inner truth. They are the secrets of the soul.

Wants whisper without license. Out of a hidden place, a

want will blurt the dare-not-say secret tucked away from view. Flashes of desire might create adverse effects because a "want" will push you to risk. Wants ask you to move out of your comfort zone and do something different. Tickets to new adventures, wants are sure to bring both challenge and change.

WANT VERSUS NEED

My friend Adrienne once remarked how much she liked a particular pen I own. It is a special ergonomically designed pen that makes writing by hand more comfortable, and it's therefore slightly more expensive than ordinary ones. When I suggested to Adrienne that she get one of these pens, since she, as a journalist, often writes by hand, she looked at me funny and said, "But I don't need it."

"Yes," I said, "but do you *want* it? I know you don't need it, but I asked about wanting. What happens to your wants?"

Adrienne had no response other than the one she had been programmed to give her entire life: If she doesn't need something, then she can't have it. Her "wants" are disqualified as extraneous, unnecessary, and superfluous.

Many people, like Adrienne, operate from a place of need. Getting their needs as opposed to their wants met is drilled into their psyches from a very early age. Somewhere along the line, they received the subtle but corrosive message that wanting is selfish, unnecessary, indulgent, and frivolous. As a result, they come to believe that they should fill their lives only with those things that they need. Because "wants" to them are extraneous luxuries that they somehow came to believe they did not deserve, they feel intense guilt whenever they allow themselves to fulfill their desires. As a result, when they do experience feelings of desire, in order to avoid the guilt feelings, they either deprive themselves or convince themselves that they actually need what they want. They rationalize their want and turn it into a need in order to justify getting it.

The basic difference between a want and a need is that needs come from a place of insufficiency, whereas wants come from a place of sufficiency. When we need something, there is a distinct absence. When we want something, we reach for something to augment or complement what we already have. Needs, of course, must be met for basic survival. But wants, also, must be met when appropriate for the sake of your happiness.

When you know what you want and you give yourself permission to have it, there is a release of delight and power that validates you as a person. This validation nourishes your self-trust, your self-confidence, your intuition, your basic belief in yourself. This reinforcement affirms your identity, your inner knowing, and your reality. Each time this cycle occurs, it strengthens your authentic self.

This does not mean that you have free license to behave in unethical, selfish, immoral, or illegal ways simply because you "want" something. It doesn't mean that your desires can operate freely without any checks, balances, or consequences. Assuming your desires are not harmful to you or anyone else and are within the parameters of the legal system and cultural mores and that they are aligned with good intention, there is no reason why you should have to deny yourself the feeling of wanting something. Nor should you deny yourself the opportunity to go out there and succeed in getting it.

HIDDEN BARRIERS TO SUCCESS

All significant battles are waged within the self.

—SHELDON KOPP

Every person has the ability and the right to succeed. Further-more, every person has a path that runs between where they are and where they want to be. If that path is clear, and you are fueled by desire, success is attainable. If your path becomes blocked, however, you will need to find and remove those bar-riers in order to complete your journey toward your finish line.

Whenever I suggest to clients that perhaps they need to look at the barriers blocking their success, they immediately enumerate all the external causes that are to blame. It is either their boss's fault that they cannot get promoted, or the bank's fault for refusing their loan for their new business, or the fault of their friends, family, or spouse for holding them back. If the success they are trying to achieve is significant weight loss, they blame their metabolism, glands, or family genes. If it is increased earnings, they blame the stock market or high inter-est rates. If it is landing a part in a movie, it is the casting di-rectors who are to blame. Strangely enough, hardly anyone ever volunteers any internal causes that might be keeping them from the success they say they want so desperately.

Marcus, a dynamic sound technician in his late twenties who had been experiencing a "run of bad luck" for several years, comes to mind. Although Marcus had a vision of a cool job earning six figures, he could not seem to hold down a job for more than six months. When I asked him what happened at the last three positions, he said the first one didn't work out because his boss was incompetent. He lost the second one because the management of the company was disorganized. The third one didn't work out because his coworkers were jealous of him and sabotaged his advancement.

Marcus overlooked the one constant in all these situations: himself. I pointed out to him that perhaps there was some value in looking within himself for any clues to a possible source of the problem rather than focusing on the immediate causes. Marcus agreed to try this, and after a short time, he revealed a fear of finally growing up. In his mind, having and sustaining a respectable, long-term job was a symbol of maturity, which in turn signaled to him the end of adolescence (and in turn, fun). Only when Marcus was able to make this connection could he work through his fear and begin to see his role in this sequence of events. He could then work toward removing the barrier that was standing in the way of him succeeding at his goal.

Self-sabotage is the number-one reason why success becomes derailed. Certainly there are such things as bad luck or unfortunate circumstances, but if you categorize those as the primary reasons why you cannot get what you want, then you are caught in an endless cycle of false causes or blaming. If there is a discrepancy between what you say you want and what you are getting, then this is a signal that you need to dig a little deeper to discover the source of your obstacles.

Imagine that you are playing tennis. You intend to hit the ball on the baseline in the left-hand corner of the court. The problem is that the ball keeps going out of the court and you repeatedly lose points. You can blame the racquet, the surface of the court, the quality of the balls, the wind, your opponent, your lack of lessons, but your shot will never change until you do something different. You must change your grip, your stance, your swing, the angle of your racquet, or the bend in your knees if you want the ball to hit the baseline. It is the discrepancy between your intention and the reality of the situation that provides the essential clue that something internal needs to be adjusted. Owning the problem is the first step toward solution.

AMBIVALENCE

Ambivalence is defined as "uncertainty or fluctuations caused by the inability to make a choice." It may sound ridiculous to suggest that you might be subconsciously rejecting what you say you want, but in the case of thwarted or derailed success, consider it a possibility. Succeeding is a loaded concept for many people, fraught with feelings of fear, anxiety, and guilt; the end result can be a deep inner schism dividing their efforts from their outcome.

You may not be conscious of having any ambivalent feelings, but that does not mean they are not lurking beneath the surface. Ambivalence is like carbon monoxide—undetectable yet deadly. Underlying doubt or uncertainty about the validity of your desires or your ability to manifest them can creep into your subconscious without your even realizing it. All that you are conscious of are frustrated attempts to arrive at your destination and the resulting disappointment that ensues.

CHANGE OF IDENTITY FEARS

Frequently our identity is wrapped up in our current state of being, which of course makes it difficult to embrace a new reality. Although you may want to succeed at whatever goal you have, you may have some difficulty if you overlook or ignore the identity changes that might come along with such a success.

Who will you be if you succeed at your goal?

Ken had been struggling financially for years. At the age of thirty-five, although he held an executive position at a sports apparel manufacturing company and earned a good salary, he was in considerable debt and frequently could not pay his monthly bills. To him, success meant being financially soluble (and hence debt-free), yet each month he seemed to dig himself deeper into a hole and drive himself further from the achievement of his goal. The situation became so familiar to Ken that he began to identify himself as a person with financial difficulties. He became accustomed to turning down invitations to accompany his friends on expensive vacations as well as being unable to take a date out for a nice dinner. Although he desperately wanted to participate in these events, he resigned himself to the fact that he was someone who simply could not afford them.

When Ken came to see me, I asked him if there might be any unconscious reason why he might not want to be financially stable. He thought about it for a while and then hesitantly volunteered a few details from his early years. When Ken was growing up, his family was comfortably middle class until his father's investments hit the jackpot when Ken was fifteen. Immediately thereafter, Ken's father announced he was leaving the family and moving in with his new girlfriend. It took years for Ken and his mother to get over the emotional loss and to get back on their feet financially, as Ken's father left them penniless.

"I guess somewhere inside me I believe that money changes everything," Ken said wryly. "Maybe I keep myself in financial straits to prevent myself from ever becoming like my father."

I nodded, cheering internally for Ken's breakthrough. He had figured out his fear with little more than a single question from me. Once he identified the fear of who he might become if he was financially solvent, he was able to work through that fear and plot a clear course to succeed at his goal.

Sometimes our fear of identity changes can be so strong that we continually set ourselves up for failure. This happens quite frequently when people aim to make personal changes, such as quitting smoking or losing weight. Their personal identity is so enmeshed in their behavior patterns that altering them is too intimidating a prospect to overcome.

Anna had been seventy pounds overweight since she was a teenager. At the age of thirty-eight, she decided finally to lose the weight that had been a source of bitter unhappiness and self-deprecation all those years. She tried diet after diet, mixing powders, blending shakes, attending meetings, and measuring portions, all to no avail. As soon as Anna made any progress toward her goal, she lost her momentum, broke her diet, and regained all the weight that she had lost and more.

Anna's big blue eyes were filled with tears as she sat across from me pouring out her story. My heart went out to her as she told me tales of being tormented in grammar school, alternately neglected and teased by boys in high school, and ashamed of herself and her body in the years since. She told me about all the diets that had ended in frustration and asked me to help her find her way out of her maze.

As I listened to Anna, I saw how she defined herself throughout the telling of her story. She consistently referred to herself as "the fat one," or "the bigger daughter," or "a heavy woman." She had spent so much time in this identity that she had no other frame of reference with which to identify herself. Her identity was so firmly wrapped up in being overweight that she did not allow any room in her subconscious mind for any new possibility. Although she might have felt unhappy about the role she played, it was the only one that was familiar to her. Losing a significant amount of weight (her definition of success) would force her to reexamine who she was in relationship to herself as well as the rest of the world; Anna was not quite prepared to do that.

Success can cause an identity crisis. It can force you to speculate on "Who will I be if . . . ?" a notion that is difficult for some to imagine. Frankly, people tend to define themselves in terms of their limitations ("the fat one," "the short guy," "the one with knock knees," "the dumb one," etc.). When forced to define themselves in terms of their successes, many people feel uncomfortable.

Did Anna begin each diet with an eye toward failing, just to avoid the discomfort of a new reality? Of course not. Anna believed with all her heart that she wanted to lose that weight. What she neglected to look at, however, was what came along with losing that weight. In other words, she overlooked the shadows her goal brought along with it. Anna needed to understand and embrace all the aspects of what it would mean to succeed at her goal before she would be able to do so.

If you are striving for success and not achieving it, ask yourself what will accompany the success you are pursuing. Will your identity, lifestyle, financial status, or the way you spend your time change? Might your friends or family treat you differently? Will you have new responsibilities that might be intimidating or overwhelming? List everything that comes to mind, no matter how ridiculous the thoughts may be. You may be surprised to discover that what is holding you back is the unconscious anticipation of the outcome of your desires.

Fear of change

Every success brings with it change. Each new level you reach, every dream you fulfill, every goal you attain causes changes, both positive and negative. The anticipation of those changes can cause fear, which in turn may cause you to unconsciously sabotage your efforts.

Philip had been working on his doctoral dissertation for two and a half years. His wife, Ellen, and he had worked out an arrangement that enabled him to do so. Ellen worked at an insurance company five days a week to support the family, while Philip worked at home on the dissertation in the mornings and looked after their seven-year-old twins every day after school. The plan was for Ellen to leave her job and return to full-time parenting once Philip finished his dissertation and went back to work. It was an arrangement that worked well, especially for Philip, who adored his sons and loved the fun-filled afternoons he spent with them building magical race cars out of boxes and playing video games.

Meanwhile, Philip was having tremendous difficulty completing his dissertation. He came to me to figure out why he was having so much trouble finishing it, since this was the only thing that stood in the way of him earning his much-desired Ph.D. and graduating.

When I asked Philip what would change when he finally did complete his thesis, it was as if a light bulb went off in his brain. "That's part of the problem!" he said excitedly. "Once I finish this, everything will change. I'll have to go get a job, and I won't get to spend time with my boys. I'll really miss them."

The barrier in Philip's way was his hesitancy to end this particular phase of their family life. Once he isolated this factor, he was able to discuss it with Ellen. The two of them made a promise to work out a new arrangement whereby Philip would still spend quality time with his sons *and* return to the workplace, as was part of their original deal. With his fear eliminated, Philip completed his dissertation within three months.

What will change in your life when you succeed? Peek under the surface and see if there is a dark side that is keeping you from succeeding at your goal. If there is, you will need to face that issue head-on and either root it out or find a creative solution, so that it will not prevent you from reaching your finish line.

LIMITING BELIEFS

"I could never . . ."
"I don't deserve . . ."
"I shouldn't . . ."
"I don't have what it takes."

Have you ever uttered any of these statements? You may have, whether you consciously recall doing so or not. Many of us are programmed with limiting beliefs about ourselves—what we can do, what we can be, what we deserve—so that breaking through those beliefs is truly significant.

Your beliefs dictate your behavior. This is true in love as well as in business and in life in general. What you believe to be true about yourself is rendered true because of the unbreakable link between your beliefs and your actions. If you believe you will fail, you will fail. Conversely, if you believe you will succeed, you will succeed. If you believe you do not deserve whatever it is you want, you will not get it. Conversely, if you believe that you deserve all the goodness that life has to offer, you will be open to receive it. If you are convinced that you don't have what it takes, you will make sure that you do not. If you believe that you have exactly what it takes, then you probably do. As Henry Ford said, "If you think you can do a thing, or think you can't do a thing, you're right." Whatever you believe about yourself and your circumstances directly impacts the reality you create in your life.

George believed that he would never become a partner in his law firm. He said he wanted it so much that his entire career depended on it. Yet his belief was stronger than his intention. He believed that he would always get passed over, that someone would be positioned more strategically and he would never be chosen. George was right. His beliefs became his self-fulfilling prophecy.

Imagine no limits

Your imagination can be used to identify and exorcise your limiting beliefs. Start by prying the sealed lid off of your dreams. Remove the internal ceiling that you have imposed on yourself, move into your imagination, and allow the child in you to dream, fantasize, and create from the place inside that feels that initial sparks of desire. Go to that childlike place where you can be, do, and have anything you want.

What do you want to be? What do you want to do? Where do you want to go? What do you want to have? Empower yourself to be bigger than you ever imagined, to do feats that you are impressed by, and to have whatever stretches your imagination.

Imagine that the world is your canvas, and you have all the tools, time, and capacity to create whatever reality your heart desires. What would the masterpiece of your existence look like?

Confronting the "yeah buts"

What will immediately surface in response to your most wild imaginings are what I call the "yeah buts." The "yeah buts" are your mind's way of protecting you from disappointment. The critic within splashes buckets of ice water on your tiny embers of desire. They act like realistic rational adults extinguishing your rediscovered possibilities. "Yeah but I'm too old. Yeah but it's too late. Yeah but I don't have the education." The list can go on and on.

Deal with the "yeah buts" one by one, strategically. For example, if a desire that arises for you is to be the CEO of your company, be prepared for the "yeah but" that says you couldn't possibly. Before giving in to that negative belief, however, take a good hard look at your vision. Is it really absurd? Is it truly so impossible? If not, would you be willing to go for it if you really, truly wanted it?

The goal of this exercise is not necessarily to force you to change your life radically, nor is it to suggest that you should abandon all reason, tie a red cape to your back, and jump off a tall building expecting to fly. Rather, the goal is to open your mind to consider possibilities. If you are to move out of "I could never" into "Yes, I *can*" and from "I don't have what it takes" to "I'm up to the challenge," then you must expand out of the limits of your decisions and beliefs.

Who knows? You might even dream up a possibility that even your most strident "yeah but" can't diminish.

EXTERNAL PRESSURES

It is a sad fact of life that not everyone cheers for each other's successes. It would be lovely to think that each person could feel content within him- or herself and not feel the need to keep or bring down others just to boost his or her own self of self-worth. Yet that is not always the case. So many people are trapped in feelings of insufficiency that they find it difficult to be gracious about other people's breakthroughs.

Those around you may have a lot invested in you being where you are in life. They may endeavor to keep you in check, ensuring that you never succeed beyond where you—or they—currently are. They may measure themselves according to where you are on your path, and if you change, that threatens their choices and lifestyles. They may feel threatened by your success and subtly try to dissuade you from pursuing your dreams. Or they may have your best interests at heart and do not want to see you set yourself up for disappointment, so they discourage you from aiming too high.

What does this have to do with your success?

Everything. When you receive messages, subtle or direct, from those close to you that you are being greedy, too ambitious, too unrealistic, or reaching too high, it takes its toll. Doubt or uncertainty may creep into your consciousness and erode your self-confidence.

Kelly and Vanessa had been best friends since high school. They had been on similar life paths since then, both moving to New York City and pursuing their careers, Kelly in fashion design and Vanessa in the culinary arts. They dreamed together about when Kelly's designs would dominate the Paris runways and Vanessa would be billed "the hottest chef in New York." Kelly would live in a huge loft in Tribeca with floor-to-ceiling windows, and Vanessa would live in a four-story townhouse just off Fifth Avenue. At the same time, they commiserated over their current low starting salaries, long hours, and difficult bosses.

Shortly after they both turned twenty-eight, Kelly left her job and went out on her own. It wasn't long before her design for a chic line of tennis wear took off, and suddenly she was inundated with orders from all over the world. Her income increased dramatically, and finally she was able to afford that loft in Tribeca she had always dreamed of. Vanessa, meanwhile, was still working at a French bistro, hoping to receive an offer from one of the upscale restaurants that would catapult her into a more prestigious realm.

Although Kelly tried hard to not make her friend feel jealous, Vanessa reacted badly. She started to call Kelly "Miss Fancy Pants" and made snide comment about the clientele that would spend their money on designer tennis clothes. Kelly had always trusted Vanessa's opinion implicitly, and thus she took her friend's comments to heart. She began to wonder if perhaps she did not deserve the success she was experiencing.

There are other instances that are far less blatant. One I see frequently is family members who do not want to see each other become disappointed, discouraging each other from setting anything but safe, sensible goals. One woman I counseled told me she did not want to encourage her son to apply for medical school because if he were rejected, he would be devastated.

Sometimes spouses can restrain each other without even realizing it. When Wendy's husband, Bob, a musician, began getting offers to play for significant venues, she found herself feeling jealous and anxious rather than happy for his success. As a result, she began taking subtle swipes at him, including saying things like "I guess you think you're too much of a star to take out the garbage now?" Bob confronted her, and she revealed a fear that Bob would become famous and leave her—and their marriage—behind. Bob assured Wendy that he loved her and would never leave, regardless of how his career went, which then enabled Wendy to offer him her encouragement and support. Now, whenever Bob plays, he feels buoyed by the sight of his wife's proud, smiling face in the front row.

Look around you. If there is anyone in your life who might be silently or verbally asking you "Who do you think you are?" be cautious. The answer they anticipate may be far less glowing and positive than the one you are striving for. Perhaps without intending to, they are asking you to stay the same, which translates into "don't grow." Tread lightly with those who may not be ready to embrace you and your dreams in all their glory. They may reach that point eventually, but in the meantime, all they are doing is keeping you from succeeding.

If you believe someone in your inner circle is trying to hold you back or keep you in check, often it helps to confront that person directly. The person may not even be aware of what he or she is doing or that his or her actions have any influence on you. More often than not, if you point out how much you need their encouragement, your loved ones will be only too happy to give it to you. They will feel like an integral part of your team and change from barriers into agents of encouragement.

CHALLENGING MEDIOCRITY

Some people see things and say, "Why?" But I dream things that never were, and I say, "Why not?" — GEORGE BERNARD SHAW

There is a point of view that claims "Life is not a bowl of cherries" and, as the classic Rolling Stones song says, "You can't always get what you want." It is a whole paradigm that people buy into as a way to accept mediocrity in their lives and rationalize not striving for more.

That paradigm is in direct opposition to three basic assumptions I have about people and their ability to succeed:

1. People have their own answers within themselves regarding what will make them happy.
2. They possess the personal power to cause those inner answers to become reality.
3. Anyone can have life be the way they want it.

These three assumptions, when held up against the negative paradigm, can feel either empowering or intimidating, depending on what you believe you deserve and which set of assumptions you operate from.

Whichever basis you come from affects the filter through which you perceive reality. If you subscribe to the negative, that is what you'll get. Argue for your limitations and eventually they will win. If you subscribe to the positive assumptions, however, you have a far greater capacity to catapult yourself higher toward your natural place up in the stars.

You can deem yourself successful whether you get the bowl of cherries or convince yourself you are content with just the pits. The real question, however, is: Will you be fulfilled by a bowl of pits?

The game of success cannot begin until you roll the dice: the dice of desire. When you allow yourself to imagine and claim the "wants" that are rightfully yours and remove the barriers standing in your way, nothing can stop you from realizing your dreams. When success is what you truly want, then you are already well on your way toward making it happen.

RULE THREE

Self-Trust Is Essential

To be fulfilled, you must know yourself
and honor your truth.

Each one of us knows what makes us feel alive. We all know on some level what makes our eyes sparkle and the fire in our bellies ignite. There isn't any mystery discovering what we enjoy and what brings us pleasure. It isn't terribly hard to unearth our talents or learn what we desire. The real challenge is trusting ourselves enough to heed those inner messages.

Knowing and trusting yourself leads you to the path that is uniquely yours. Honoring that truth gives you the greatest chance of succeeding, for it is when you are aligned with your truth and act upon those inner signposts that you are living authentically and up to your highest potential. Authenticity and alignment with inner truth begin with the seed of self-trust.

Self-trust is needed not only to guide you to your authentic path; it is needed to keep you there when the road gets bumpy. It is needed when inner doubts arise along the way, when others think you are "crazy" for wanting what you want or doing what you do, when you need to make tough choices, and when you encounter trials and obstacles. When you trust yourself, you are able to decide the best course of action for yourself from that place within you that just simply *knows*. Self-trust emanates from your gut and can be tapped only after you truly know, accept, and honor your authentic and essential core.

Your truth is a source of power. When you align with who you are, you enliven yourself. Every step you take is either toward your truth or away from it. Each step you take toward it energizes you; each step you take away from it robs you of energy. When there is a discrepancy between what you know to be your truth and the various concessions you make, a schism is created. Energy is required to maintain that schism, which keeps you from accelerating toward your desired outcomes or goals in life. Hence, the closer you stay within the bounds of your truth, the sooner you will find the fulfillment you seek.

Uncovering Your
Essential Self

To rise to the top, you must first get to the bottom of things.
— Robert C. Savage

The discovery of your essential self comes after digging down through the many layers of the imagined self: your persona, the façade, who you think you are, who you wish you were, who you are afraid you might be.

Finding your true self means connecting with your essence. It means believing and telling the truth about who you are and who you are not. Doing so may be simple or painful, depending how in touch with reality you already are. Finding your true self is critical to success because it is what allows you to align with your authentic path: the one that will lead to fulfillment.

Knowing who you are allows you to tap into your inner desires, from which you can then plot your course. When you know who you are, you know what you want. When you know what you want, you open yourself to the possibility of choice, the place where you connect with the path that is right for you.

The driving force behind the discovery of this path is your purpose. Why are you here? What is your mission? What do you want your life to be about? What contribution do you want to make to the world? What legacy do you want to leave behind? When you uncover your essential self, you can know the answers to all these questions and find your true calling.

DISCOVERING YOUR PURPOSE

Some people know their purpose from a very early age. A friend of mine tells stories about himself as a young boy toting a miniature toy briefcase to school each day. He was the one in his second-grade class picture wearing a suit and tie, along with a rather serious expression. He laughs about it now but admits that from the time he was very young he always knew he wanted to be a "businessman." At the age of seven he didn't know exactly what that meant, but he always saw himself taking a train into "the city" with a briefcase, just like his father. That calling never left him. He went on to major in business administration in college, earn his MBA, and is now the managing director of an international jewelry business. He still, of course, carries a briefcase, only now it is large enough to carry his laptop computer.

Other people take years to discover their purpose. These are the majority of people. They are the ones who have more self-discovery still ahead—perhaps like you—who are trying to make their way through the maze of skills, preferences, expectations, and fears.

An exercise that we have done in team-building training sessions for decades has proven to be a helpful tool for excavating individuals' driving purposes. Essentially, it is a simulation of a survival setting. Try to imagine yourself in a situation in which life as you know it has been pared down to the essentials of food, water, shelter, and basic survival. You can imagine that you have been on a ship that has been lost at sea and you end up on a deserted island, or with a wilderness expedition that lost contact with the base camp, or as a survivor in the aftermath of an earthquake. The particular disaster is not what is important; what is important is imagining that you have limited resources and you must solve the problem of stabilizing the people, strategizing an action plan, and figuring out how to return people to their families and homes.

You are among twenty-five survivors. Roles have not been designated, and it is up to each one of you to decide what you must do individually and collectively to get back to your homes and families. You have a certain amount of water and various supplies with which to stay alive while you plan your strategy. The exercise helps people see what they innately do without the comforts of modern life.

Ask yourself: What role you would play? What would you naturally be inclined to do in this situation? Do you organize, strategize, or delegate, or do you jump in and help others? Do you focus on finding out people's strengths and dividing them into teams, or do you proceed as if everyone is responsible for him- or herself? Would you focus on supplies, shelter, clothing, or would your priority be to nourish the survivors? Do you automatically check to see if anyone is injured? Are you concerned about people's mental and emotional well-being and try to help?

I have seen a wide variety of responses while conducting this exercise. Some people automatically take charge while others naturally support. Some start organizing the supplies and others assess the geography, climate, and natural resources. Still others look at ways to communicate with the outside world. Some immediately address safety issues while others focus on calming, curing, and care taking of the survivors. Still others focus on shelter and hygiene issues, while others are concerned about safeguarding against predators.

One woman said she would appoint herself the historian and begin recording everything that each person said and did as well as writing down what they learned and how their new systems progressed. This was very interesting, because in her regular life, she was a sales clerk in a clothing store who secretly always longed to write for a newspaper.

Another said she would establish a barter system so that everyone could trade what they had for what they needed. Not surprisingly, she is studying for her MBA.

A man said he would build shelters to house everyone. In real life, he was an architect who used this exercise to confirm that he loved creating structures.

Someone else said he would immediately help everyone cope with their emotions, the fear and anxiety of being separated from families and friends. Shortly after doing this exercise, this man went back to school to get his master's degree in clinical sociology. This exercise helps people get back to basics and connect with their essential purpose.

What would you do? To what would you be instinctively drawn? What activity would you automatically tackle? What task beckons to you? What is your primary concern? If you can imagine yourself in these circumstances and answer these questions, then you will almost certainly come up with some clues about your natural proclivities.

FINDING YOUR PATH

Follow your inner moonlight.

—ALLEN GINSBERG

The formula to find your path to fulfillment is astonishingly simple: Follow your preferences, and they will lead you to your path. Find what brings you joy and satisfaction, and trust that it will also bring you prosperity. Find what makes your blood boil, and trust that it will also fuel your existence. Discover what makes your heart sing, and trust that it will create music in your life. In other words, find what matters to you, and trust that it is the signpost you have been looking for.

FOLLOWING YOUR HEART

Larry was a terrific landscaper. He had been working with the soil ever since his early twenties, when he took a part-time job as a landscaper to finance graduate school. He loved the smell of fresh-cut grass, the sound of crunching gravel, the challenge of a empty yard, and the delight in his clients' faces when they saw their property transformed into something beautiful.

When Larry completed graduate school, he expected to pursue his chosen field, psychology. Larry discovered, however, that he was saddened at the thought of leaving the landscaping that he dearly loved. He knew he would miss the satisfaction he got from working outdoors, being close to the earth, using his aesthetics, and creating something with his own hands. He postponed finding a job or beginning a counseling practice for close to a year before he admitted to himself that his real love was gardens and yards, not counseling. He now owns his own landscaping business and sleeps contentedly each night knowing he is doing what is in his heart. He also uses the communication skills he learned in his counseling training to help his clients make choices about their gardens.

Throughout her childhood, Ginny loved arts and crafts. She was great with a glue gun and created all kinds of gifts for her family and friends. As she grew, up, she continued to learn about craft techniques. Ginny also loved weddings. She thought that the union between a man and a woman was the greatest moment in life. As time went by, her path became clear. She merged her two loves and started a business creating wedding accessories. First Ginny designed them, then she trained others how to make them. Glue gun at her side, she took it to the altar. Ten years later the company is grossing $1 million a month. Not so bad for a glue-gun girl with weddings on her mind.

Drew sold medical supplies for a living. He was capable, but his heart wasn't truly in it. He was fascinated by the stock market and often could be found checking the stock pages or watching to see where the Dow closed at the end of the day. Finally, Drew decided he knew enough about the market to make a go of it, so he left his job and started day-trading. He's not a millionaire, but he is paying his bills and having the time of his life.

Sometimes passion comes from an innate talent or interest, as with Larry, Ginny, and Drew, or sometimes it comes from a life event that happens without warning. A woman, Candy

Lightner, who experienced one of the greatest tragedies one can endure—the death of her child at the hands of a drunken driver—decided to make it her life mission to prevent this from happening to other children. She founded MADD, Mothers Against Drunk Driving, a well-known organization that lobbies against the combination of drinking and driving. Because of Candy and MADD, more teenagers and adults now appoint designated drivers on evenings out, and as a result millions of lives are saved.

Alice was a breast cancer survivor. Like so many other women she knew in that circumstance, her contact with medical professionals was distressing. Because of this experience, she became personally committed to changing the way doctors and nurses interact with cancer patients. Today she heads up a breast cancer organization that also lobbies for political reforms in the medical and pharmaceutical industries. She supports women with breast cancer physically, emotionally, psychologically, and at times even financially. Her crisis became her life's work.

Still others find their purpose because of a childhood experience that left an indelible impression on them. Many people who become pediatricians credit their own early experiences—both positive and negative—with medical care as the inspiration for doing what they do. Dave Thomas, the founder and owner of Wendy's, grew up in rather unhappy circumstances. The only warm family experiences he recalls are when he and his adoptive father ate at restaurants and Dave could watch other happy families around them enjoying meals together. Out of that particular memory arose one of the most successful fast food chains in the country.

Your heart is your life force. It pumps blood throughout your system, blood that enables you to live. In addition, your spiritual heart unlocks the key to your motivation. It is the seat of inspiration and passion. It is your true guide to the future. Follow your heart and it will point you toward the place in the sun that is rightfully yours.

What is your heart telling you?

Are you ready to listen?

Will you trust what you hear?

IDENTIFYING YOUR GIFTS

Do you run like the wind or play the saxophone with gusto? Do you prepare meals with love or take photographs that inspire? Do you have an eye for color, wrap presents beautifully, or take charge easily? Do you have a knack for numbers, or are you a masterful communicator? Do you have an ear for languages, a nose for perfume, or a touch that heals? Are you clever with finances or a whiz at organization? Can you hit a baseball out of the park or dance with grace?

The answers to these questions are your clues to your gifts and your path. Knowing your gifts—your talents, your assets, and your abilities—is the first valuable step in knowing what path will work for you. Doing that which you excel at is a major ingredient in your recipe for future success.

When I was twenty-five I found out that I had a gift for asking questions. Not only did people open up and begin to share with the open-ended questions I asked, but they also felt safe enough to tell me truths they rarely divulged to anyone else. I thought that this was normal. I thought that anyone could do it. I thought that moments of awakening happened all the time in other people's presence.

It was not until my dear friend Kathy pointed out to me that few people can extract deep truths and inspire epiphanies in others that I understood that, in fact, I had a gift. Kathy knew her gift was to play piano by ear and entertain friends with her music. She pointed out that one of my special gifts was to create a safe environment in which people can discover and reveal their inner truths. Once I acknowledged my gift, I started to use it. I stopped denying that I was good at something and I started contributing to the lives of others in a way that was deeply fulfilling.

So many people, when asked what they are gifted at, reply either "I don't know" or "Nothing." Yet they almost always overlook their natural gifts because they are simply too close to them to see objective reality. Think about it: Is there anyone you know who isn't at least good at *one* thing? Everyone has something unique to offer, whether they are ready or not to admit it to themselves, their inner circle, and the world.

The writer Sue Bender suggested "Perhaps our natural gifts elude us because they are so obvious." If you cannot readily identify your gifts, ask those in your inner circle to do it for you. Most likely they will be all too willing to illuminate for you the unique talents and abilities you have to offer.

Do you have a gift that you conceal, deny, discredit, or brush aside? Have you embraced what you have to give? Are you ready and willing to tell the truth about what you have to offer?

KNOWING YOUR NEEDS

Every person has individual requirements in order to thrive. You can have the highest-paying, most exciting job in the world, but if you would prefer to be in a more laid-back, non-profit position, chances are you will not flourish. Just as you would not blossom in a love affair with someone who was not right for you, you cannot succeed to your highest potential if you are in circumstances that do not resonate with your specific needs.

There are many factors to consider when you look at your personal requirements. There is environment, pace, pressure level, time considerations, and level of flexibility. There are elements such as visual needs, auditory tolerance, tactile surroundings, and even scent sensitivities to take into account. Of course, there is also the question of roles, in terms of a call to leadership as opposed to a support position.

Sometimes finding your personal preference is a process of trial and error. One of the best ways to determine the working scenario that is best for you is to look back at your history and sift through the factors.

Begin by recalling those times in your life that you were at your peak performance. Write down what about each of these experiences that you think worked best for you. Most likely you will begin to see threads of commonality between those experiences in which you felt the most alive.

For example, Ben recalled that he felt the most like himself at three points in his past: when he worked as a camp counselor at the age of eighteen, when he worked as a ski instructor at the age of twenty-two, and, surprisingly, whenever he was doing yardwork around the house. As soon as he identified these three experiences, he immediately recognized that he was at his best when working outdoors.

From there you can begin to define that place where you thrive. Consider these factors:

1. Do you like working alone or as part of a team?
2. Do you like trying new things, or do you prefer a routine?
3. Do you enjoy flexible hours or feel more comfortable with a daily structure?
4. Do you resent or appreciate authority figures (bosses, mentors, etc.)?
5. Do you prefer multiple tasks or a single point of focus?
6. Do you prefer to consider people's opinions or work solely from your own?
7. Do you show up early, or are you always rushing to be on time?
8. Do you produce your best quality of work in the morning, the afternoon, or late at night?
9. Is visual stimulation important to you?
10. Do you thrive when the pressure is on, or are you better in a calm atmosphere?
11. Do you feel more energized outdoors, or are you more comfortable inside?
12. Do you prefer to be active or easygoing?

Some of these questions will cause habits to surface, others will point out preferences, and some are simply personality traits. All, however, are important to consider when you imagine the path for you. When you are working from within your optimum circumstances, you eliminate the negative factors that interrupt your sense of flow.

When I was in my early twenties, before I knew what I wanted to do, I took a part-time job at a large cosmetics company. My job was to sit in a small, cagelike room high above the store and wait for money to be sent up via a vacuum tube. Since I was handling large sums of cash, there were protective bars on all four sides of this room and of course no window. All day long I waited for the capsule of money to zoom in. Then I took out the money, logged it and put it in the safe, gave the proper change and receipt, returned the tube, and waited to do it again.

By the end of the fourth day, I was a zombie. I feel stimulated around people, and I also enjoy lots of mobility, so needless to say, this was not the ideal job for me. There was no way I could survive in this setting, let alone thrive. With encouragement from my sister, who knew me and my needs well, I quit and never looked back.

Going against your grain will inevitably cause discomfort. Jody, for example, was sensitive to noise. She lived on the nineteenth floor of an apartment building in New York City, and in order to sleep at night, she needed to install soundproof windows to drown out the honking cars below. She bought herself a special clock that woke her up to the sound of rolling waves rather than the blare of an ear-shattering alarm, so as to not awaken each morning with her jangled nerves.

Yet despite all the care she took at home, Jody went to work each day as an assistant to a record executive at a music label. She was excellent at what she did, but her daily existence was a strain. All day long the people around her played their radios, each one tuned to a different station. Between the blaring mix of music, the constant ringing of the phones and fax machine right near her desk, Jody left the office each night tense and depleted. She often needed to go home and put an ice pack on her head to ease her tension headache.

Clearly, this was not an optimal situation for Jody to flourish in. She eventually spoke to the human resource director and was able to transfer to the classical music division of the label, where the noise level was far less jarring. The phones rang less, and the department head had a policy that nobody could play music above a certain level. In this environment, Jody's natural abilities were able to shine through.

Roberto by nature is an independent spirit. He was never particularly good at teamwork, mostly because he did not like to be slowed down by others' opinions or ideas. When Roberto joined the creative department at an advertising agency, problems arose for him from the get-go. He tried to suppress his independent nature because he thought the way to get ahead in advertising was to work at a big firm, but in the end, he only ended up frustrating his boss and himself.

Roberto arrived late, if at all, to most department meetings. He interrupted his colleagues when they spoke because he was confident that his ideas were superior. When a project was assigned to the department, Roberto would immediately go off and begin creating whatever came to his mind. He did not wait to see what others thought, nor did he participate in the division of responsibilities. Although Roberto usually produced brilliant work, he did so at the expense of his coworkers' feelings and his manager's patience.

After eight months, Roberto and his boss mutually agreed that he did not belong in the job he was in. The company valued his work, however, and agreed to employ him as a freelancer. Now Roberto is free to create products according to his timetable, without having to accommodate colleagues or to work within the confines of a team setting.

Determining what is true about you is part of knowing who you are. When you know what is true about you, you can create situations that are optimum for your satisfaction and peak performance.

TRUSTING YOUR INSTINCTS

When I speak to college students, they invariably say things to me like "I am planning to go to law school, but I don't plan to practice. Do you think I should take three years to do that?" or "I'm interested in teaching. Is that what I should pursue?" or "I think I want to counsel criminals. Do you think I'm crazy?" or "I love to write music, but I don't know whether to focus on hip-hop or jazz. What do you think?"

Most of these students have an inkling of what they would like to do but are afraid to trust what they feel. Some have so many things that they are interested in that they feel overwhelmed and afraid of making the wrong choice and going in the wrong direction. They ask my advice mainly because they are looking for permission to trust themselves. What I really hear them saying is "I don't want to make a mistake. Can you help me feel more comfortable with my choice?" "I'm afraid of making a mistake—of going in the wrong direction—of wasting time. I'm afraid that, someday in the future, I might regret the path I choose today." The underlying message they are conveying is that they are afraid to trust themselves.

Where the fear comes from

No child is ever born afraid. Fear is a learned behavior. You learn to be afraid when you feel insufficient, when you feel you can't cope, when you perceive danger, and when your needs are not met. You learn fear when you feel alone and are unable to care for yourself. As people mature, the world subtly teaches them to doubt their own instincts and question their abilities. They stop trusting themselves. When plans don't work out as expected, people begin to question their choices. Hence self-confidence may become shaken. We all want to make the right choices and avoid as many mistakes as possible.

The college students who ask me questions about their career choices are looking at a world in which they are told they will change careers at least six times, a world that is rapidly changing, a world of uncertainty with no guarantees. They are looking at a world of downsizing, restructuring, mergers, and acquisitions. They see relatives and friends jobless after decades of service. People entering the workforce are questioning what they have to offer and what is being offered to them in return.

Given all of this, I certainly cannot fault these students for being apprehensive about their futures. What I can do, however, is remind them that the only thing they can rely on in this changing world is themselves. Remembering that is the most direct route back to self-trust.

Trust versus fear

Trust and fear are antithetical. Where one exists, the other is either blocked or absent. If you are afraid, you cannot trust your choices. Conversely, if you are in "trust" with yourself, then you will not be afraid of the choices you make.

Trust in an inner glimmer that lets you know you are on track. When you trust yourself, you pay attention to the spark you feel inside. You know that your instincts and intuition are to be honored. You are willing to take action, even if the action you take comes with no guarantees.

Fear creeps in when you doubt yourself, when you dwell on the worst that can happen, when you focus on outcomes that will be detrimental to you. Fear perches itself at the edge of your consciousness, waiting for the smallest invitation to enter. The only way to keep it at bay is to remain firmly rooted in self-trust.

If you find yourself leaning toward fear, you may want to consider taking some time and space to realign with your core. You can use whatever method works best for you—meditation, a walk alone in the park, talking to a trusted friend, doing an activity that you love. When you remember your unique talents, abilities, and true worth, you will see the fear evaporate as quickly as it arose.

"Right" versus "wrong" choices

Sometimes we don't understand or we forget that there are no mistakes, only lessons. This is especially difficult for college students embarking on their first big decisions in life. The objective of fulfillment is not about doing everything perfectly and avoiding all mistakes. It's about making choices from the clearest place you know, then backing that choice and riding it out to see where it takes you.

So how do you know which choices are the right ones and which are the wrong ones?

You don't. You just make the choice that feels right to you at that time, and you follow that route either toward success or toward the lessons you were meant to learn. On the road to your destination, you will certainly learn about yourself, other people, and about life in general. There may be times, when and if you choose, that you revise your map or change your destination entirely. This doesn't mean that you made the wrong choice to begin with or that you failed in your pursuits. Rather, it means that you wisely altered your original plan once you had more data.

I recently consulted a woman named Audrey who complained about being a failure. I asked her what led her to believe this was true. She said, "I'm thirty-five years old and I still haven't landed. I still don't know what I want. I go from one job to another, from one place to another, and none of them end up being 'it.' "

I asked Audrey to list each job she had held from the very first one, as a baby-sitter, to her most recent, as an administrative assistant to a mortgage broker. As she reviewed the chronology of events in her mind, I asked her what she liked about each position and what she didn't like. I also asked what she learned and why she left each position. As she was speaking I took copious notes. When she completed her story and her observations, I read over all I had written and commented, "I don't see anything here that remotely hints at failure. I heard a story about a person who learned a great deal about a variety of fields; you stayed long enough to learn what was there for you. You left as soon as you learned what you were there to learn. I see no failure in that."

Audrey sat in amazed silence. She knew I was right, but she had never viewed her life from that perspective. She realized that the way she is was a matter of choice. The question was: Did she prefer to notice what was right about her choices or what was wrong?

There is no such thing as a useless mistake. The "wrong turns" you take in the road are merely chances to view scenery you would not have seen had you remained on the straight course. When you trust yourself and your ability to persevere and survive setbacks, choosing your path will seem like a far less daunting task.

Changing Direction

Let your soul stand cool and composed before a million universes.

—Walt Whitman

Over the years I have consulted with thousands of people who sat before me with tears in their eyes admitting that the path they are on is not the right one for them. So many are lost in the list of their skill sets, the golden handcuffs, the expectations of those around them, and the secret knowledge that they do not belong in the life they are in.

Many already know the truth deep inside. They know what it is that would fulfill them, but there is a deep fear of honoring their own truth. They dismiss the small voice inside that tells them what would be right for them, usually out of inse-curity or external pressure not to do so. The kernel within each of their stories is a need to honor who they really are.

THE EXPECTATIONS OF OTHERS

Josh, thirty-four, was an attorney for the federal government. He was good at his job and worked hard every year. After ten years, he sat in my office admitting the truth for the first time.

"I hate my job," he confessed. "I really dislike being a lawyer, and I don't like the legal system in general." He said he dreaded going to work every day and was mildly depressed most of the time. I asked Josh why he became a lawyer. His re-sponse was that he did it for his dad, a high-profile attorney in the district attorney's office. Josh dearly wanted his father's ap-proval and becoming an attorney was one sure way to ensure that he would always be in good favor.

When I probed further and asked what he enjoyed, he said, "I like working with my hands. I like tinkering with gears and chains." I must have looked quizzical because he explained, "Bicycles, I love to work on bikes and motorcycles. I like grease on my hands. I like the smell of oil." I was astonished but tried to conceal my amazement. Isn't it interesting that someone can spend ten years doing something he doesn't like to do merely to gain the approval of another? It is amazing but not shocking. In fact, it happens every day.

The key that unlocks the prison of external expectations is the willingness to tell the truth to yourself, to your family and friends, and to the whole world. Your gut feeling should be what is in the driver's seat, not other people's expectations. If you give others the power to dictate your path, you are merely a passive participant in your own life. There are two choices: being the driver or the passenger.

Which one will it be?

Drowning out the negaholics

Negaholics exist. They are the naysayers who have mantras of "can't," "shouldn't," "it won't work," "it's not possible." They are the people in your life who encourage you to stay small and play it safe, and who project their expectations onto you. They believe they are realists only saving you from disappointment, but in reality they are risk-averse. Their intentions may be good, but they unwittingly rob you of the freedom to use your own instincts as your rudder.

You need to become strong enough to be able to deal with them when they attack your dream. Dreams can be fragile when exposed to the harsh light of the outside world, and you may need to protect your most precious ones. The following list of exercises will help you with your mental fitness program, so that you can stay centered in your beliefs and not stray off course.

1. Put up notes of self-encouragement on the refrigerator, the bathroom mirror, your dresser, your desk, and the corner of your computer screen. Seeing these messages written down will encode your mind to embrace them.

2. Read biographies and short stories of people who have dealt with and overcome adversity. Have two to three pages as your bedtime reading, so that you can stay inspired.

3. Surround yourself with people who believe in you. If you notice negaholics, train them regarding your expectations, negotiate about how they speak to you, or evict them from your life.

4. Organize your support team and tell them exactly what you want from them. Request your biggest supporters to remind you daily of your goal and encourage you to do it.

5. Write out your vision and mission, and refer to it each morning when you awaken, to program yourself for the day.

6. Anticipate negattacks, and prepare for how to address them when they happen. What will you say? How will you respond? It helps to have a response ready and waiting so that you are not caught off guard. What will you tell yourself to stay centered?

Let's take Josh from the above story as an example of how this works. When Josh decided finally to leave the practice of law and learn more about working with bicycles, he put Post-it notes up on all the mirrors in his house with positive affirmations. He wrote things like "I can do it!" and "It is important that I do what I love, not what my father loves." Seeing these small notes of encouragement every time he looked at his reflection reinforced his self-confidence.

He collected biographies of some of the people he admired, including the Wright Brothers, who gave humans wings despite all evidence and belief that they could not do so, and Lance Armstrong, the American who overcame a 30 percent chance of survival from cancer and went on to win the

Tour de France in 1999 and 2000. He read these over and over to keep himself inspired.

He told his closest friends of his plans and asked them to refrain from their usual custom of joking about serious subjects. He also asked Lisa, his girlfriend, to remind him that he was loved *no matter what he did for a living*.

He wrote his mission and vision on a piece of paper and read it out loud to himself every morning and evening to reinforce what he was doing.

Last and, in Josh's case, most important, he practiced what he would say when his father expressed disappointment or disapproval. Whenever his father made noises about the amount of money he had spent on Josh's law school education and "respectable" careers, Josh would take a deep breath and say to his father, "I understand that you have your perspective, and I respect it. However, I also need to respect my own preferences, and I hope you can, too." He also would silently remind himself that his father was only trying to show him love, albeit through control, and that he was grateful to have a father who cared so much.

About two years after all this happened, I ran into Josh and asked him how he and his father were doing. He grinned and told me he had given his father a high-tech mountain bike for his last birthday and that the two of them now go out riding every Sunday. Whenever they pass someone by the side of the trail whose bike has been damaged, Josh's father is the first to pull over, offer Josh's mechanical services, and give one of Josh's cards.

THE GOLDEN HANDCUFFS

Paul came to see me because he was unhappy. He expressed shame admitting the fact that even though he earned well over six figures a year, had an enormous house, four cars, and an art collection worth a considerable amount, he wasn't happy. As an executive vice president at a bank, he was entitled to many perks, including the use of the company condo in Jamaica and a car and driver to take him to work and other luxuries. Given all this, Paul felt like he had no right to be dissatisfied. But he was.

Paul woke up each day with a low-grade malaise. He went through his daily routines, sensing that there was something slightly off in his life, but couldn't put his finger on it. When I asked Paul if there was something he would rather be doing, he immediately retorted, "It wouldn't matter anyway. I can't even think about changing careers. I have a mortgage, car payments, country club dues, and other bills to pay. I can't make any changes with all those responsibilities."

"Maybe not," I said, "but what good is the house, the cars, or the country club if you don't enjoy them?"

Paul was a prisoner of golden handcuffs. He would not allow himself to imagine that there was another way or that he could take control of his situation. He was so attached to his lifestyle that he neglected to monitor his internal well-being.

As it turned out, there was something Paul wanted to do more than being a banker. Paul wanted to be an art dealer. He loved his collection and believed he had a good eye for new talent. It was not until many months later, however, that Paul returned to talk to me about making a change. He needed to wait until his dissatisfaction outweighed his creature comforts from his material possessions. New possibilities are not visible when you are a prisoner of harmony.

It is now five years later, and Paul has become a successful art dealer, making close to the same salary he was making before. Only now the income brings him joy rather than binding him to his life.

Is your lifestyle keeping you bound to a life path that is not right for you? If it is, your only escape is to bravely break out of the handcuffs and embrace the challenge of a new possibility. It is not easy to take such action, but no one ever said fulfillment comes easily.

Trust that what you built once, you can build again. If you were smart enough, strong enough, and determined enough to create a comfortable lifestyle for yourself doing something you didn't like, imagine what you can create for yourself if you are doing something that you love.

The possibilities are endless!

CLIMBING OUT OF THE RUT

So often people are trapped in their web of dissatisfaction. They complain about the life they are living, yet they do nothing about it. We all know someone who sincerely believes there is nothing that can be done to improve his or her circumstances. These people say things like "It's too late to start over," or "I can't afford a pay cut," or "I'm already too far in debt to make any changes now." They may not know it consciously, but they have dug themselves into a ditch of negativity surrounded by barriers built out of familiarity and comfort.

You know when there is a gnawing feeling inside. You know

when you are just biding your time—getting through the day, the week, the month, the quarter. You know when there is something missing in your life. When awareness of this feeling surfaces, you have one of two choices: You can try to ignore it and stay rooted in your misery, or you can change things.

The way out of the web of dissatisfaction is by taking the brave first step of admitting the truth to yourself. If you continue to live in denial, telling yourself that "fine" is enough for you, then that is all you will ever receive. If you are hiding from your truth, you can never change anything. Telling the truth helps you get unstuck.

Once you acknowledge your truth, you can follow the four remaining steps toward creating change, if you so choose. They are: choice (actively selecting to release the pattern), strategy (creating a realistic plan), commitment (taking action), and celebration (rewarding yourself for succeeding).

The pivotal element you need to climb out of your rut is willingness. Without the willingness to improve your circumstances, you cannot muster the energy and creativity you will need to change your life.

Are you willing to make a change for the better, or would you rather stay where you are? Remember, what you make of your life is up to you.

BELIEVING IN YOURSELF

Nothing is at last sacred but the integrity of our own mind.
— RALPH WALDO EMERSON

When you believe in yourself, you are able to make authentic choices. Trusting yourself allows you to act with boldness, to have faith in your ideas and abilities, to innately know that you will do what is right for you.

So many of the great achievers of our time were labeled out of their minds for the visions they had or the abilities they banked their futures on. Amelia Earhart was scoffed at for simply suggesting a woman could fly a plane as well as a man. A good majority of Thomas Edison's ideas were perceived as ridiculous, even impossible. When Katharine Graham, the legendary publisher who published *The Pentagon Papers* and Woodward and Bernstein's historic Watergate stories, first took over the *Washington Post*, it was widely believed that she would fail. All these people shared a deep belief in what they envisioned along with the courage to trust themselves. They had the willingness to follow their inner radar at all costs.

The only difference between these people and you is that their accomplishments have already been recorded, while yours are in the making. We all have the potential for greatness, including you. The place to begin is by tapping the internal source of greatness: confidence.

CONFIDENCE

Confidence is inner faith. It is a feeling of sureness in your bones that you have what it takes to accomplish whatever task you set out to perform. There is a unique and powerful feeling that comes as a result of knowing you can count on yourself.

We are all born with an innate sense of confidence. It is a natural state of being. This is why children are so sure of themselves and often appear arrogant and undaunted, even invincible. If a baby didn't have confidence, it wouldn't even try to stand up. Babies come from an inner knowingness that signals them that they can make those rubbery limbs into working tools of transportation.

This innate confidence gets squashed down as the years go by, as we hear "No," "Don't touch that," "You're too young," "Don't be ridiculous." Actual experience teaches us that there are things that are beyond our capabilities. By the time we mature into adults, our reserve of confidence may have become so depleted that we have trouble accessing it.

So how can you find your way back?

There are two ways to regain your lost intrinsic confidence: inner exploration and outer imprinting. Socrates believed in the power of inner knowing, whereas Aristotle believed external imprinting was needed in order to grow and learn. They were both right, because Socrates was addressing the soul and Aristotle was dealing with the mind.

To strengthen your inner knowing, you will need to experience small successes as a way to rebuild what was torn down. Let's imagine your task is to build a house. Such a task might seem daunting if you have never done it before, and hence you may not feel confident about your ability to do it. The secret is to begin with something small, like laying one single brick. When you do that successfully, you begin to build confidence. The second, third, and fourth brick increase it further, and then you begin to harness that momentum into a sense of "I can do this." Before you know it, you are not just laying bricks; you are building a home.

In order to augment and complement the sense of accomplishment that begins to resurface within you, you also will need external support and motivation. As Aristotle suggested, look around you. Look at those who have succeeded before you and borrow confidence from them. Learn from their actions as well as their mistakes. Use them as role models and their accomplishments as mirrors for your own unfulfilled potential.

Nicholas was a screenwriter. Despite several near misses, he had not yet been able to sell any of his screenplays. For two years he lived off his savings and continued to send query letters to agents and producers while taking classes in the evening and continuing to hone his skills. By the end of the first year, his friends and family began questioning him about how long he was going to give this "experiment in creativity." By the time the end of the second year rolled around, most of them were telling him he was being foolish to continue his pursuit and encouraged him to find a good-paying job.

Nicholas, however, refused to give up until he saw his dream realized. He *knew* that he would be able to sell one of his screenplays some day. Part of his determination came from sheer perseverance, but the majority of it came from an inner resolve to back his choice to pursue screenwriting. He trusted his talent as well as his ability to market himself and learn from past mistakes.

When Nicholas felt those inevitable moments of self-doubt creep in, he would remind himself of success stories like James Cameron's *Titanic*. Even though all of Hollywood thought he was crazy for investing so many millions into a movie in which everyone already knew the ending, James Cameron plowed ahead. Whenever the negaholics or internal doubts started to get to Nicholas, he reminded himself (and them) that *Titanic*, which was the biggest-grossing movie of all time, would never have made it to the silver screen if it were not for James Cameron's confidence and perseverance.

Thankfully, the story has a happy ending, as Nicholas sold one of his early screenplays (for a large sum of money), and a major studio plans to produce it as a feature film within the next few years.

There are no guarantees in life. Nicholas might not have sold his screenplay, after all, but he never would have known if he hadn't given himself a chance. If you trust yourself, you naturally put all of your energy behind your choice. When you stand behind your choices, your chances for success are multiplied. Success comes from committing to your choice with every fiber of your being. If you have faith in yourself and back your choices, you will see the return of your investment of time, energy, effort, and capital.

Within each one of us there is a spiritual DNA, a code that depicts our strengths, talents, preferences, and passions. The spiritual DNA must be decoded if we are to unravel our life's purpose. We succeed when we fulfill our purpose. The challenge presented to each one of us is to discover the path that is unique to us and to trust ourselves so that we may follow it and achieve our individual dreams.

When you trust yourself, you discover your truth. When you honor that truth, you can see your authentic path. Following your authentic path will lead you to the vision of prosperity that ultimately will engage your mind, ignite your heart, and cause your soul to sing.

RULE FOUR

Goals Are the Stepping-Stones on Your Path

Your journey to fulfillment is propelled forward
by the goals you set along the way.

Your path to fulfillment is carved by your dreams, paved with your gifts and talents, and forged by your determination. What propels you along are the goals that you set along the way. They act as stepping-stones on your path, each one a marker of where to step next on your journey toward fulfillment.

A goal is a way of determining where you are headed. It is the "there" that you identify from your vantage point of "here." Between where you are and where you want to go is an invisible cord; when you stake out and define where it is you want to go, you energize that cord. The promise of the fulfillment of your goals is what creates the dynamic tension that pulls you toward their realization.

We all have visions: what we want to accomplish, what we want to achieve or attain, images of how we would like our lives to be. What transforms those visions into reality is the willingness to formulate them into real goals. By doing this, you begin to chart a course that will take you to the heart of your highest visions and dreams and make them real.

The Power of Goals

I know of no more encouraging fact than the unquestionable ability of man to elevate his life by conscious endeavor.

— Henry David Thoreau

"Goal setting" has become a rather overused term in the fields of career and life guidance, but there's no way around it: It is still the most effective way to get you from where you are now to where you want to go. Conventional wisdom may seem ordinary, but the power of its effectiveness lies in its universality.

I have been using goals with my clients and myself for almost three decades, and I know that the process works. It works by having you articulate your wishes and desires, by being exceptionally clear and specific, and by being brave enough to attach a date. All the people whom I have midwifed to success have started the process by establishing their goals. If they didn't have a goal, I never would have known how to support them, nor would they have known what steps to take and when to take them.

Your goals are what move you along your personal game board of success. As you achieve each one of your goals, you move yourself closer to the vision of success that you have created in your mind's eye. Goals are mileposts along the road that help motivate you as you reach for your finish line. The size and scope of the goals are not important—they can be small or significant; what matters most is that you take the time to articulate them.

Without goals, you find yourself hoping things will happen. You may cross your fingers, wish as you blow an eyelash, and open fortune cookies anticipating confirmation of your unspoken hopes. "Starlight, starbright, the first star I see tonight . . ." may feel like a magical way to make your dreams come true, but it is hardly a reliable method for getting what you want in life. As Benjamin Franklin said, "He that lives upon hope will die fasting."

Achieving your goals will not only motivate you, it also will keep you focused and on course, thus preventing you from going around in circles. My friend David Campbell said, "If you don't know where you are going, you'll probably end up somewhere else." How can you know where you are going or how you will get there if you don't have a clear destination in mind?

VISIONS VERSUS GOALS

Dreams pass into the reality of action. From the action stems the
dream again; and this interdependence produces the highest form
of living.
                                                    —ANAÏS NIN

When I ask people what their goals are, they often say things
like "to be happy," "to be healthy," "to make a million dollars," or "to find a wonderful relationship." They make grand,
sweeping generalizations about where they envision themselves, how they want to live, what they want to be, do, or have.
Most are surprised when I tell them that what they communi-
cated are not, in fact, goals. What they are communicating are
wishes, intentions, and visions.

Goals and visions are first cousins. They are in the same
family but have some distinct features that set them apart.
What they share in common is that they both describe what
people want and what they picture in their mind's eye. Both
are optimistic portraits of what people desire. Yet there is one
big difference between the two: Visions are general, and goals
are specific.

Visions describe how you see yourself in the big picture. In
Rule One, the images you created are visions. They provide the
inner landscape of your desires; they act as a compass guiding
you in the direction that you want to go. They are lofty, overarching statements of intent. They are generally characterized
by the silent echo of "someday."

Goals, on the other hand, are tangible. They are dated, specific, targeted, and measurable. Goals are statements of calcu-

lable results to be achieved. They provide a means for translating wishes into actual results, by grounding you in reality. They help people know when they "win" and provide a basis for determining where effort should be concentrated. They are what transform "someday" into "today."

Visions are important in order to formulate your big picture and encourage you to stretch your imagination to encompass what you can be. They are the raw material of dreams. Visions are larger than life and provide something to aspire to; however, you can wrap your arms around your goals. Visions are the canvas; goals are the actual brush strokes you make to paint the picture of your life.

For example, Ali had been dreaming about owning a ski house for years. She loved to ski and also loved to spend time in Colorado. Owning a cabin somewhere near a mountain was a definite "must" for her in terms of her overall life plan. Yet as each ski season came and went, Ali continued to do nothing to transform that vision into reality.

What could Ali have done? What goals might she have set to begin the process of owning this dream home?

Well, for starters, she might have set a goal to organize her finances within the next six months so that she could begin saving for the house. Or, if she already had the money in the bank, she could have given herself tasks, such as to make appointments with at least three brokers before the end of the next season. Anything—even the smallest goal, like committing to one particular town before the following year—would have sufficed. The point is to establish a firm, specific finish line that you actually plan and are able to cross.

Mike, on the other hand, had a vision that was quite

common: He wanted to be rich. Since he was a little boy, Mike dreamed of a six-figure bank balance, luxury cars, a large house that included a swimming pool, plenty of room for guests, and a closet full of designer suits. His tastes ran toward the extravagant, and he had a vision of himself living in this manner.

The reality of Mike's situation, however, was quite different. He lived in a modest two-bedroom house, drove a leased midsize car, bought most of his clothing on sale at the local men's store, and his bank balance rarely exceeded four figures.

For Mike to transform his vision into reality, he needed to start with some basic goals. His goal could be to receive a raise, create a financial plan, or look for a higher-paying job. He could execute some tasks to move the ball down the field. For instance, he could visit a financial planner, ask for a raise, or look for a new job. He could even set himself a simple goal, like saving enough extra cash to buy one designer tie. One small realized task would most likely unleash enough personal satisfaction to fuel and launch him toward bigger ones.

Look at the following visions and the potential goals that could be set to realize each vision. By doing so you can get a better sense of the difference between visions and goals and how you personally can begin to translate your own visions into goals and then reality:

Visions Versus Goals

VISION	GOAL
To live by the ocean	To live in a cottage in Malibu by the year 2002
To be a leader of my industry	To be quoted in the *Wall Street Journal* within the next five years
To get married	To find a loving, fulfilling, committed, and long-lasting relationship with a significant person whom I am attracted to and in love with by next Valentine's Day
To get in shape	To weigh 175 pounds, be firm and fit by June 15
To be financially independent	To be debt-free and investing $500 per month by the end of 2005
To have a baby	To visit the doctor and find out all I need to know about getting pregnant by the end of next month
To find a better, more fulfilling job	To be actively employed doing what I love to do and able to support myself in my desired lifestyle before I turn forty

To own my own business	To research franchise opportunities and choose one by the end of the year
To work with children	To volunteer at my local hospital one day each week, reading to the children in the pediatric ward
To write a book	To create an outline for my espionage novel in time to submit it for consideration in the writers' group starting this fall

Which of your personal visions are you ready to translate into reality? Which one can you envision yourself breaking down into confrontable goals? It might be one of these, or it might be something entirely different and unique. Chances are, you already know which vision of yours you are secretly itching to pursue. If you don't, here is a hint: It is the one that is whispering to you in those quiet moments, the one that tugs at the edges of your soul, and probably the one you are most afraid to admit to yourself. That's the one on your runway, waiting to take flight if you will only recognize it on your radar screen.

SETTING GOALS

Light tomorrow with today!
—ELIZABETH BARRETT BROWNING

The act of setting goals provides you with two valuable assets: a sense of causality and the stepping-stones to illuminate your path. Goals put you at the helm of your life; pursuing them acknowledges your causality in your situation. They allow you to steer your course rather than simply drifting along and letting life happen to you.

Setting goals sounds fairly easy, but for most people it can be quite challenging. Setting a goal can be unsettling, because it means setting up the possibility of disappointing either yourself or someone else. All fear of failure can be avoided if you never establish any goals at all. After all, you can't fail if you never state what you want to achieve.

THE NOT-NOW SYNDROME

One of the things that my clients and friends both love and hate me for is the fact that upon hearing them express a vision, I immediately ask, "When would you like to do that?" I do this because I am eager to see them have what they want. I know the only way this happens is through commitment.

I had a conversation with my dear friend Dolores. We started discussing her wishes, dreams, and goals.

"Someday I would really like to have a sport utility vehicle," she said.

I responded with my usual "When would you like to have it?"

"Oh, someday. I'm in no hurry," she replied.

Of course, I probed. "When?"

She stood her ground and responded, "When I can afford one."

"When might that be?" I encouraged.

"When the time is right." She defied my probe.

"Ideally when would you like to have it?" I persisted. (Love me or hate me, I rarely give up when it comes to things like this!)

"Oh, I don't know," she lamented, "not now, but someday."

I switched gears and asked her what she was feeling.

She replied, "Pressured."

I asked her why and she said, "Because I know I want one, but I don't want to put a date on it."

Again I asked, "Why?"

"Because it depends on a lot of different factors."

I knew we were getting somewhere with that statement. "Like what?" I persisted. "Well, for instance," she said, "part of the vision of owning the SUV is having a country house to drive it to on the weekends. Right now I don't have a house; I don't even have the down payment. I know these cars are expensive and I simply can't afford one. So without the house or the money to buy the car, it's stupid for me to set a date."

Listening to Dolores reminded me of hundreds of clients who are reticent to formulate a goal without the bank account to realize the dream instantly. I let her in on one of the secrets of goal setting: Establishing the goal is a step in and of itself; it doesn't mean that you harvest the goal immediately. Setting a goal is like planting a seed. You put it out there, then you water it, give it sunlight, and nurture it. Sometime in the future a shoot emerges. You continue the caretaking process until you have a strong, sturdy plant with blossoms and/or fruit. You don't plant a seed and stare at the ground waiting for instant results.

This conversation was a revelation to Dolores. Previously she had thought that if she set a goal without the resources, she was kidding herself. She believed that "not now, but someday" was telling the truth and being realistic. She had no idea that she was involved in a self-defeating cycle, teasing herself with a sort of, maybe wish.

Like Dolores, many people suffer from what I call the not-now syndrome. Those who are afflicted are held back either by their fear of failing to get what they want or by their fear of actually getting what they want. It may sound bizarre, but there is a lot of truth to this.

Every now and then, each of us benefits from a healthy dose of the not-now syndrome. These are the moments when your eyes are bigger than your wallet, or your dreams are larger than your life can contain at the moment. You cannot take that trip to China if you only have $250 in the bank and no credit left on your credit card; nor can you become CEO of an entertainment conglomerate if you are still a freshman in college. There is a right time for everything; the key is knowing when to set a date in the future, to make your goal concrete, as opposed to putting it off out of fear.

If there is a dream you are postponing transforming into a real goal, ask yourself what it is that is standing in your way. If the response sounds like a list of excuses rather than legitimate, realistic facts, you have your answer. It's time to break out of the not-now syndrome and assign some realistic dates to those future dreams.

Smart Goals

You might notice in the visions versus goals chart that all of the goals share five criteria: They are specific, measurable, attainable, realistic, and time-based. An easy way to remember these is the acronym SMART. In order for goals to be within your reach, they need to be SMART ones. If a goal is not SMART, it is not a goal; it is merely an intention.

To turn your wishes into goals, it helps to begin by running them through the five different criteria to ensure your best chances of success with your endeavor. These criteria serve as a matrix through which you put your goals to see if they withstand the sifting process and a few hardy reality checks.

1. **Is your goal** *specific?* To make your wish specific, you must articulate precisely what you mean and *exactly* what it is that you want to achieve. For instance, if your goal is to climb the corporate ladder within your company, you need to articulate what that means for you. Perhaps your goal is to become president of the company eventually. Or, another example I recently heard from a workshop participant, if your wish is to play professional basketball, you might specify which position you want to play and for which team.

2. **Is your goal** *measurable?* The second criterion is that it must be measurable. You must be able to count, or

mark, the outcome in some way. In the corporate situation, the marker would be your appointment by the board to the position of president. On the basketball court, it would be getting drafted to play for the Lakers or whatever team you prefer.

3. **Is it *attainable*?** The third criterion is that it must be attainable according to your personal profile. Is it possible for you given your features, characteristics, assets, and limitations to achieve this goal? Let's face it, you can't be five feet tall and realistically play center for a major league basketball team. If your firm requires all executives to have a college degree, you can't expect to become president of the company without one. In other words, the goals must be within your realm of capabilities.

4. **Is it *realistic*?** Is it realistic for you to play professional ball if you have bad knees? Is it realistic for you to become president of your company if you know it means relocating to another continent despite aging parents who require your care and attention? In other words, does your goal make sense? There is a fine line between reaching for the stars and losing your grip on reality. The best way to test to see if your goal is realistic is to notice how you present it to yourself or to others. If you are defensive about your goal, it probably lacks realism.

Some people can defy reality. They can make what seem like totally unrealistic goals become reality, which is extraordinary. Anne Sullivan helping Helen Keller to communicate without the ability to speak, see, or hear was something close to a miracle. If you believe in your heart that you have the capacity to make miracles happen, then, by all means, set extraordinary goals. It is up to you to determine your capacity to stay the course, remain diligent, and stay committed to your goal no matter what. Realistic is your subjective assessment.

Rudy Ruettiger was one of those committed people. His goal was to play football for Notre Dame. It was one of the most unrealistic goals imaginable. He was short, lightweight, poor, and didn't have the grade point average to be admitted. He was relentless in the pursuit of his goal. He learned to compensate for dyslexia and persisted in his athletic efforts. He finally was admitted, received a scholarship, and through a series of circumstances actually played on the playing field with the team for all of thirty seconds. Both the book and the movie *Rudy* were inspiring because of Rudy's indefatigable commitment to his completely unrealistic goal.

If this sounds like you, then go for it. If, however, you would rather set reality-based goals, then keep that in mind.

5. **Is your goal** *time-based*? Fifth, you want to anchor your statement of outcome in a time frame. Every goal must have a completion date attached. If a date is not attached, the desired outcome turns into an intention rather than a goal, postponed by the eternal promise of "someday," crippled by the not-now syndrome. Dates commit intentions to calendar realities. They target the time frame for the goal and prevent it from withering away into infinity.

For instance, if you intend to be president of your company but don't specify when you plan to achieve this, the process can drag on forever. In fact, you can even postpone striving for it, since there is no deadline for the outcome of your efforts. You can always put your master plan for advancement into effect tomorrow, after all. What's the rush about today?

If you don't put a date on being on the basketball court, you could find yourself eligible for a senior citizen's pass before you realize that your chance has passed you by. When I last checked, the Lakers didn't have any players over sixty-five.

A note about the time-based factor: You can always revise deadlines, as needed. You aren't a failure if you don't meet your goal by the date you originally set. It is wise to assess your timetable periodically and determine whether the time frame you set is still appropriate. If it isn't, you can change it as necessary. Failure comes when you don't allow yourself the flexibility to alter, edit, and revise your goals when necessary.

Even the best-laid plans need alteration from time to time. General Motors planned to have the first electric car—the EVI—ready for mass production with the new extended battery in mid-1999. The company ran into snags with the technology and the date was extended to the beginning of 2000. As one of America's corporate giants, GM knows when to revise deadlines as needed and doesn't hesitate to do so if that is what is called for.

Missing a target doesn't mean that you failed; it means that you must tell the truth, reevaluate, and set another date, which, it is hoped, is more realistic.

USING THE SMART MATRIX

Eric came to me because he was unsure whether to leave his job as a college biology professor and pursue his love of the outdoors. He wanted to start a small business leading people on hikes through the Blue Ridge Mountains. He had hiked most of his life, knew those trails backward and forward, and also knew a great deal about the area's indigenous flora and fauna. He was excited to combine his hiking experience with his knowledge and teach those he guided.

I told Eric about the SMART goals matrix and suggested that we run his vision through it to see if it withstood the tests. He agreed, and so we first looked at whether his goal was specific. It was. It would not have been if Eric had only said he wanted to do something in the outdoors. As Eric knew exactly what he wanted to do within that context, we checked that one off.

Next we asked if his goal was measurable. Was there a way to measure or mark its accomplishment? Eric thought about it for a moment, then replied, "When I have at least five people registered for an excursion." This was his way to measure his accomplishment; hence, the goal was measurable.

The next question was whether the goal was attainable. Did Eric have the physical skills to lead people through the mountains? Yes. Did he have the mental capability to market and run his small business? Yes. Did he have the emotional wherewithal to take the risk? Eric paused for no more than five seconds before giving a resounding "Yes!" According to the criterion, Eric's goal was within his capacity, and hence was attainable.

Fourth, we questioned whether his goal was realistic. That one was—and always is—a little more difficult to assess. One person looking at Eric's situation from the outside might say that he was crazy to leave a tenured position at a respectable institution and head for the hills. To that person, his goal would be far from realistic. Another person who embraces the spirit of adventure might strongly disagree and think Eric's goal was well within the boundaries of pragmatism. "Realistic" can be an entirely subjective concept, so only Eric could assess whether his goal was reasonable or not.

He looked at his life circumstances and noted that there was nothing standing in his way. His wife wholeheartedly supported Eric's decision either way, his children's college funds were already allocated, and he could always fall back on teaching if his excursion business did not work out. Regardless of how much thought Eric put into this, he could not talk himself out of his dream. It tugged at him, nudged him, and tickled his imagination relentlessly. It stood up to the test of SMART goals, and he had a fallback plan.

Finally, we discussed the time-based criterion. Until that point, Eric hadn't set a deadline, for the same reason that so many people never do: fear. I asked him if he was willing to take the final step into making his goal realizable. Eric didn't even hesitate. "Absolutely! I aim to put this plan into action and leave my job at the university at the end of this term."

"What about when you plan to lead your first excursion?" I pressed.

"I want to have my first group organized and ready to go by next spring. Will you come along as my guest?"

I laughed and congratulated Eric for his bravery and enthusiasm. By making his goal meet all five criteria, he was already well on his way to winning his personal game of success.

What goals are you pursuing? Do they stand up to the SMART test? Use the matrix to determine whether the goals you are striving for are worth pursuing or need some revising. Write down your vision, translate it into goals, and run it by the SMART matrix. Remember, the SMARTer your goals, the higher the probability of your success.

Visions, wishes, intentions, and dreams are all valuable. They are what spark your imagination and encourage you to define where you want to go. In order to get there, however, you will need to bring your larger-than-life images down to earth and make a few plans. Setting goals is the first step in the creation of those plans.

Visions live in the mind; goals exist in reality. Visions give you hope; goals give you results. Visions point to a lofty tomorrow, but goals are what provide you with tangible achievements today.

While both are important, goals are what jump-start your plans into forward motion.

Are you ready to begin transforming your visions into reality?

Rule Five

Your Actions Affect
Your Outcomes

The quality and quantity of energy you put forth
directly impact the results you receive.

Everything around you, in your personal as well as your professional life, is a result of actions that you have taken. With the rare exception of gifts and miracles, everything that you pride yourself on, the achievements that give you a sense of accomplishment, the relationships that bring you the most joy, the material possessions and the experiences that delight you above all others are a direct result of your efforts to procure them.

You have probably heard the cliché "You reap what you sow"; in the arena of success, this has a particular ring of truth to it. What you put forth has a direct correlation to what you receive in return. You make things happen in your life, and you dictate how strong your chances of succeeding are. You cannot take home the brass ring if you don't board the carousel and try your hardest to reach for it.

CAUSALITY

Life is something like a trumpet. If you don't put anything in, you won't get anything out. —W. C. HANDY

Causality is the act of bringing something into existence through your own efforts. It is the acceptance and acknowledgment that you cause your reality, that what you say, do, and think directly affects the results you produce.

Causality means you are willing to invest yourself totally in what you want in order to make it happen. It means that you are willing to find the way, willing to invest the time and energy to create your preferred reality. The polar opposite to causality is "doing nothing." There is, of course, a time and a place for doing nothing, but when you are focused on succeeding, causality works better than "doing nothing." If you want to succeed, you can, of course, simply wait for the universe to deliver it to you. Or you can rely on yourself and *make* it happen.

When I was in graduate school, I had a conversation with Joe Nordstrom, the CEO of Nordstrom department store. In the conversation, he told me the following story: The salespeople in the hosiery department in one of his stores noticed that business was really slow. Although the store was normally filled with customers, recently, no one was buying socks or stockings.

One salesperson became tired of sitting and waiting for customers to show up and decided to try a completely new approach. She filled a basket with pantyhose and socks and went to a large office building nearby. She walked from office to office and quickly sold all of her merchandise. Her colleagues became excited and followed her lead. Each one chose a different office building and took merchandise to the grateful office workers. They sold basketsful of socks and pantyhose and had a great time.

I commended Joe on his management style, and he replied, "We empower our employees to go outside the box and come up with innovative, fun, and interesting ways to do their jobs rather than just sitting there waiting for customers." Both Joe Nordstrom and the company as a whole understand the value of causality. As a result, Nordstrom is one of the most successful department stores in the country.

Success comes not only to those who pursue it but also to those who go out and make it happen. The people who step up to the plate and actually swing the bat are the ones who are in the game and ultimately the ones who score.

If you don't swing at the ball, how can you ever expect to hit a home run?

Are You Betting on Luck?

We all know the fantasy: You are going about the business of your daily life when the doorbell suddenly rings. You swing open the door to discover Ed McMahon beaming at you, standing on your front steps handing you a check for $1 million.

Could this be you? Certainly, if you are the one lucky person out of every billion or so people who wins the lottery. If it is, many congratulations! If it is not, however, and your goal is to have that kind of money in the bank, then you will have to go out and earn it with your own hands, heart, talent, and brains.

If you are betting on luck, good fortune, or it being your turn, you might hit the jackpot. Then again, you may not. However, if you go after your goals the old-fashioned way— by putting forth effort and work—you come out ahead even if accomplishing your goals eludes you. You learn valuable lessons about yourself, you gain insight and knowledge, and you make a deposit in your self-worth bank.

Fate may wave its magic wand; it happens now and then. But look around you: How many people that you deem successful got there through luck alone? Did Bill Gates' empire happen without years of time and energy expended? Did Bruce Springsteen become one of the most famous entertainers in the world merely because of good fortune? Did Barbara Walters become one of the most influential journalists in America because of luck? Yes, an element of being in the right place at the right time comes into play in all these scenarios, but there was more: There was extraordinary effort.

Cal always had led a somewhat charmed life. Things always seemed to work out for him. In fact, that was a familiar mantra in his family: "Everything always works out for Cal." He had made every team he tried out for in high school, got accepted to the college and medical schools of his choice, and was offered a coveted internship immediately upon graduation. Life was pretty smooth for Cal.

That is, until he realized that he did not want to practice medicine but to follow his heart's calling and work in the sports industry. So he left his job with enough money in savings to support himself for a while. He started talking to people in sports-related industries to determine what he wanted to do and to let people know that he was looking. Cal was confident that, as always, things would work out for him.

The problem was that "putting the word out" was all that Cal did. He sent a few resumes here and there, but the majority of his efforts went into hoping that someone would call him and offer him a job.

Six months into Cal's job search he came to see me to see if there might be another approach. I asked him what his primary course of action had been, and when he told me "talking to different people," I immediately saw the problem. I shared with him an ancient Chinese proverb that seemed appropriate: "Talk doesn't cook rice."

Cal was waiting for his usual run of luck to kick in. When it didn't, he found himself, for the first time in his life, in a position where he had to take full responsibility for what he wanted and make it happen. We mapped out a more strategic and aggressive game plan, and six weeks later Cal found a job at a sports marketing firm.

Luck is a wonderful thing. However, by its very nature it comes with no guarantees. If what you are looking for is actual realization of your goals, you can *hope* for luck, but that's probably not your best bet.

Luck can and does run out. Luck keeps you hoping for

some external granting of fortune. Establishing your goals and making them happen puts the power in your hands. Besides, you won't need to look over your shoulder perpetually, wondering if you still have the luck you once had or worrying about when it might disappear. If you don't feel the power of your own causality, your vehicle will never feel fully stable and within your control.

TAKING ACTION

A journey of a thousand miles must begin with a single step.

— LAO-TZU

Goals are merely a list of good wishes and intentions until you take them forward into action. The more intellectual and reasonable you are, the easier it is to analyze the situation and avoid taking action. This is often referred to as analysis paralysis, which is where you think about something, analyze it, understand it, conduct research, discuss it with friends and family, and mull it over without ever actually doing anything about it.

In a workshop which I have been conducting for twenty-five years, titled the Inner Negotiation Workshop, I teach participants to tune in and hear their intuitive "messages" from within themselves. These "messages" provide inner imperatives about what they need to do. Hearing these messages is not all that difficult, since most people can identify those internal hunches or feelings if they are willing to listen.

Acting on their "messages," on the other hand, usually requires a risk, so that part can be a bit more challenging. As a result, we frequently observe people trying to make their message/risk more rational. They try to reason with their inner guidance. They try to find a way to negotiate an alternative that will require less action and more analysis. If they are true "thinkers," they will try to work everything out in their minds, planning, anticipating outcomes, reviewing contingency plans, trying to have everything perfect before they do anything. It never works. At a certain point, they discover that no amount of cognition will ever make anything physically happen.

After about a day or so it is usually necessary to issue an ultimatum. The leaders say something like "Either you can think about your message, or you can do it. It is as simple as that. If you have given your item sufficient thinking time, then this may be the moment to do something about it. Remember, if you are thinking, you are not doing."

The thinkers usually recognize themselves, but the words don't make jumping off the diving board any easier. Therefore, facilitators meet with the participants one on one to help make the transition from thinking to doing easier. The role of the facilitators is to encourage the participants and help them take their first step. The first step is always the hardest. With a helping hand, venturing forward always becomes a little easier.

When you shift from thinking to doing, you draw a line in the sand and say to yourself, "When I cross this line, I will start doing and stop thinking." As you cross the line, you move the molecules within you and you start to stir the world around you as well. In order to manifest the success you want in any area of your life, you must first start the wheels of action moving.

I met with Cindy, whose inner "message" revealed that she wanted to become a nurse. She confessed that this had been something she had been pulled toward for years but always cast the dream aside. Every time she got close to imagining that perhaps she could make this dream real, she would be rendered immobile. Cindy often visualized herself working in a hospital and caring for patients, but she never actually did anything to make it happen.

The first thing Cindy and I did was exorcise her "yeah buts"—all the reasons she believed she couldn't be a nurse and why her circumstances made this prohibitive. After getting all of the "yeah buts" on the table, Cindy examined them and saw that none was insurmountable. She was able to see that by clinging to these negaholic thoughts, she could safely keep herself in the analysis stage and never be compelled to take any steps forward.

Cindy drew her line in the sand. She knew she had been lingering in "thinking" mode far too long, and if she didn't do something now, she probably never would. So together we made a list of ten action items that Cindy said she could commit herself to doing, including researching local nursing schools and telling her current employer that she was going to be making a life change in the near future.

Sometimes it takes only a little bit of encouragement for people to awaken the dream, some collaborative coaching to strategize the action plan, but when it comes to deployment, that is up to the individual person. No one can move your feet forward except you.

The launch into action is what makes the difference between spectators and players on the field. Without action, you are not in the game; you are merely observing and waiting for it to begin. The shift from spectator to participant starts with a single step—into motion.

The Question of "How"

The question I am asked most frequently when it comes to getting from where you are to where you want to go is: "I want to, but *how* do I do it?"

My immediate response is consistent: Don't focus on how, focus on *what*. *How* drives you into your head trying to untangle the mystery of the act; *what* moves you into action steps that you can take. *How* is intangible and elusive; *what* leads you to the concrete, specific steps you actually can take to transform your goal into reality.

Think about it this way: If I were to ask you how you breathe, what would you say? Chances are you would pause, think, concentrate on your nose, lungs, and study the inhalation and exhalation of air. You might observe the process and try to find the appropriate words to describe what you were experiencing, or you might find a medical book that provides a clear explanation. Most people have difficulty articulating *how* they do something, because answering *how* requires analysis. Understanding *how* to breathe is not required for you *to* breathe. Doing does not require understanding. In order for you to do, you must know *what*.

Imagine that I asked you not how but *what* you do when you breathe. You would likely say something to the effect that you pull air in through your nostrils until you feel that you have taken in enough, then you exhale, and then you repeat the process. The "what" part of the question leads you to the steps in the process; how just leaves you wandering in the mysterious realm of the unknown.

Most of the things you do everyday, you do without any knowledge or understanding of how you do them. How do you talk on the phone? How do you fly on a jet? How do you cook with a microwave? In order to do these activities, you do not need to understand *how*, you just need to know what the steps are to perform the task. There is, of course, value in exploring the "how" of our universe, but when you are trying to effect results in your life, such exploration is more of a deterrent than a necessity.

If you are ready to take action, don't get paralyzed by how. Move your attention to the immediate what. In other words, bypass the bigger philosophical question and go right into the process of doing.

Mapping Out the Steps

Imagine that your assignment was to read *War and Peace*. This is an exceptionally long book, and tackling it might seem like a daunting task. It might be overwhelming to imagine reading 1456 pages. However, if you start with just one page—just one!—you will be in the process. You don't need to read the entire book in one day. Reading it one page at a time will still get the job done.

The following steps will help you design any action plan you want to make. They will show you how to break down your goal into do-able tasks, each one of which will bring you one step closer to success.

1. Make lists of all the possible things that you can do to take your wish forward. Include all the steps, from tiny to monumental. Writing them down does not necessarily mean you have to do them all, so be brave and write everything you can imagine *someone* doing to take action on making a goal like yours come true.

2. Find the one action step that jumps off the page at you. This is the one that looks the most interesting or attractive. If nothing jumps off the page, choose the one that looks the easiest to get done—the least intimidating, the one that doesn't bark back at you. It could be the smallest, simplest incremental step that will allow you to feel a sense of achievement. It is important to feel as if you moved the process forward, regardless of how insignificant the action item may appear.

   Starting with small steps isn't because you aren't able to handle anything that is more challenging, but because it will help your self-confidence to see immediate results. Self-confidence is built on many tiny moments of positive outcomes, forward movement that shows that you are "doing" something. Set your standard or task at a confrontable level so that you experience your ability. You want to jump-start your

"I can" mode so that it engages. When you get on an I-can-do-this roll, you gain momentum and build your accomplishment list.

3. Then do the first step that you have selected.

4. Celebrate that you did something that started your process in motion. Even if your acknowledgment is a momentary pause to pat yourself on the back mentally, don't take for granted the step that you finally took.

5. Keep on going. Choose another step, and then another. Each accomplishment generates energy. The greater the momentum you build, the greater the forward thrust. Each time you generate energy with your success, use it to motivate yourself for the next challenge. Motivation comes from success. You need to experience succeeding at something—even something small—in order to feel motivated to go on and do the next item on your list.

When you hit a snag, you have to go back to the moment just prior to the snag. Ask yourself what happened in that sequence of moments. Ask what created the disruption. Then deal with it, and do one of two things: Either fix the snag by trying again, or step back and tackle something easier. It might simply be the wrong time to be tackling that specific step.

For example, Bruce wanted to open a gourmet cheese shop. He began mapping out his action plan by listing the following possibilities that he could do in order to set the process in motion:

- Research the leading cheese shops in the country.
- Buy books on how to start a small retail business.
- Make contact with the cheese suppliers throughout the country to assess which ones he would want to do business with.
- Read the real estate section of the newspaper to get a sense of what it would cost to rent a storefront.
- Write a business plan.
- Go to the bank and apply for a small business loan.

Since the first item seemed to be the one that was the most appealing and the one that was the least threatening, Bruce began with that. After a month's time, he had accumulated a lot of information and felt that he had a fairly good understanding of the competition. The wheels were in motion, and he was inspired to keep on going.

Next he went out and bought a stack of books on everything from raising capital to insurance. He read all of them, and his knowledge base grew. Now Bruce knew not only what it would take to compete in the business but what it would take to start his own cheese shop.

Then Bruce felt confident enough to begin drafting a business plan. As he made his way through it, the old echoes of doubt started to ricochet in his mind again, and he felt his confidence faltering. Upon hitting this snag, Bruce assessed what went wrong. He realized that he had jumped into the realm of finances before having a firm enough grasp on how much money he actually would need. Writing a business plan at that point was dealing in abstract and intimidating terms, and that took the steam out of his momentum.

So Bruce changed course and chose another step that would keep his I-can energy building. He started researching real estate opportunities in town. Upon discovering that he needed to raise less capital than he had originally thought, he returned to his business plan and tackled it.

And so it went, until Bruce was approved for a small business loan. He opened his shop a year later and views the entire experience as one big lesson in causality.

All that is required to move into action is that you venture forth, step by step. If you continue taking steps that you can handle and putting one foot in front of the other, eventually you will reach your destination.

WHAT IT TAKES

Life engenders life. Energy creates energy. It is by spending oneself that one becomes rich. — SARAH BERNHARDT

What does it take to succeed? Is there a set formula through which we are guaranteed success?

The answer to the second question, of course, is "no." If there were, everyone would be able to follow the formula and actualize all of his or her dreams.

While the first question, "What does it take to succeed?" does not have an absolute answer, there are some behaviors that do lead to success. Over the years I have coached many individuals and companies to the threshold of success. The people who consistently win all tend to share three common behaviors: diligence, focusing on quality of effort not just quantity, and the willingness to give 100 percent.

DILIGENCE

Diligence means applying yourself to what you are doing. It is carving out the time and dedicating the energy to do the necessary work that is required. In its simplest form, it is rolling up your sleeves and getting down to business.

Doing diligence means that you do what you need to do without procrastinating, making excuses, or looking for shortcuts. Those who are diligent are focused on the task at hand. How much attention and dedication you give your efforts correlates directly with the results you receive in return.

If you wanted to take a vacation, for example, diligence would require you to research airfares, hotels, and rental cars. After the research, you would need to make the reservations, pack, and make sure you reached the airport, with your ticket, in time for your flight. If you missed any of these steps, you might miss your vacation or find yourself having to camp out on the beach after you arrive.

In life, your goals may require that you strategize, visualize, try different approaches, reassess, and persevere. Some goals will demand a lot from you, some a little. Regardless of what is called for, your challenge is to meet the mark and deliver.

GENERATING QUALITY

Everywhere we turn these days, we are inundated with advertisements for products and services from car rentals, to diamond pendants, to toothpaste. Each advertisement tries to convince the consumer, through slogans, jingles, and smiling celebrities, that its product or service is superior to all the others. While the sheer number of advertisements can seem overwhelming, their underlying message actually is helpful to remember: Quality counts.

It counts in terms of effort, as well. There is a difference between logging hours and putting in productive time, just as there is a difference between working hard and working well. The former is spinning your wheels; the latter is striving for excellence.

When you put forth quality, the universe responds in kind and returns that level of commitment to you. When you cut corners, save pennies, and sacrifice the integrity of your product, service, or efforts, the results will reflect that.

Beth made cookies for a living. She was a fantastic baker, and several of the larger restaurants in her city ordered her cookies on a regular basis. When someone asked her the secret to her success, I wasn't surprised at her response:

"I don't cut corners anywhere. I only use the freshest and best ingredients. I pay a delivery person top dollar to ensure all my deliveries get there on time, if not early. I never send a batch of cookies out the door that is less than what I want it to be."

I asked Beth about her work ethic, and not surprisingly, she set the same standards for herself as she did for her cookies.

Be mindful of the quality of your efforts. Halfhearted efforts yield mediocre results. Excellent efforts, however, yield impressive ones.

GIVING 100 PERCENT

The U.S. Army has had the slogan for many years "Be all that you can be." This slogan is simple yet compelling because it is an invitation to fulfill your potential. If you give 100 percent of yourself to your endeavor, you can never look back with regret. After all, if you give your all, there is nothing more you could have done.

Giving 100 percent means going the extra mile when you need to. It means being resourceful when necessary, learning what you need to in order to succeed at your endeavors, following up, following through, and following the process to its conclusion. When you put forth 100 percent, you use all your talents, the power of your mind, your efforts, and your passion to bring about success.

Jonathan wanted to get promoted. There was a position opening up in the near future that he had his sights on, and he deployed a strategic action plan to make that job his. He started by writing a memo to his boss about why he wanted the position; in it he built a case for why he was the best person to fill the job. He included all the reasons why he was not only qualified for the position but deserving of it.

Jonathan did not stop there. He contacted the person who had held that position previously, who had moved on to another company, and interviewed her about the ins and outs of the job. When he discovered that running meetings was a large part of the role, Jonathan offered to run a meeting at the company the next time one was scheduled, to show management that he was up to the challenge.

He continued to follow up with his immediate boss and wrote a memo to the directors explaining the new initiatives he would implement if given the opportunity. Not surprisingly, Jonathan got the promotion.

You know when you are giving 100 percent. You can feel it in your bones and in every fiber of your being. When you are fully aligned with your goal and do whatever it takes to make it a reality, you become a powerful force to be reckoned with.

Success is like a mirror: It reflects back to you exactly what you hold up before it. That which you embody and deploy will appear before you as tangible results; that which you strive for can show up in the looking glass only if you make it so.

What you do and how you do it will determine your ratio of success. If you truly want to succeed, assess how much time, effort, and energy it will take and do it. The results you will see will be well worth it.

RULE SIX

=====

Opportunities Will
Be Presented

=====

There will be moments in life when you are presented
with new options. What you choose in those moments
is up to you.

n opportunity is a moment in time when there is
an opening for a new possibility that had not previously been considered. It is a moment of choice,
when a new option is presented to you. It is the intersection
between where you are and a new road. Which way you turn is
up to you.

In those moments you are faced with a decision. Either you
can stay on the road you have been on and continue toward
where you were going, or you can make a change, try a new
road, and see where it takes you. Without the foreknowledge

=====

of what each route will bring, which no one except psychics possess, neither one is better than the other. Each one contains its own value, whether through fulfillment or in lessons to grow from. The challenge presented to you is to weigh every option, make your choice, and then direct your vehicle in the direction you select.

Imagine that you're cruising along the highway of life, setting your course, moving forward, focusing on your destination. Suddenly you see an exit looming before you that catches your eye and beckons. It looks attractive, like a fun detour, with promises of adventure, new vistas, excitement, and possible treats. What do you do? Do you immediately exit the highway? Do you dismiss this diversion as off purpose and remain on course? Do you slow down and pull over to the shoulder of the road to think it through? Or do you panic with indecision, hit the brakes, and cause a traffic jam behind you?

Each alluring exit is an opportunity. These exits on the highway of your life might not necessarily be opportunities worth taking, but they are opportunities all the same. The key here is that something new has entered the scenario.

Everyone knows people who have stories about a missed opportunity about which they kick themselves. There is the person who didn't buy Microsoft stock in the early 1980s because it was too risky; another who turned down a part in what is now one of the longest-running plays on Broadway because she was certain it would flop; and still another who shied away from the Internet because he thought it would never catch on.

Then there are others who seized what they believed to be sparkling opportunities, only to discover that they mined fool's gold instead. There was the gentleman who invested heavily in what was to become a waterfront shopping arcade who lost it all when the builder absconded with the money; the airline pilot who quit his job to become a private instructor who discovered that he had little to no teaching ability; and the graphics designer who accepted a high-profile assignment that took a tremendous toll on her private life.

Could any of these people have decided differently? Perhaps, knowing what they know now. But there is no magic formula to ensure you take only the opportunities that pay off. The best you can do is gather the data, learn from your past choices, observe the choices of others, and then rely on your intuition and your knowledge to help you make your next choice.

RECOGNIZING OPPORTUNITIES

. . . from the sky, from the earth, from a scrap of paper, from a passing shape, from a spider's web . . . We must pick out what is good for us where we can find it. —PABLO PICASSO

There are two kinds of opportunities in life: the glaringly obvious ones and the hidden ones. The obvious ones are things like the promotion for the job you have been seeking, the offer for an exciting new job, a marriage proposal from the person you love and want to spend your life with, or an apartment offered in the city where you have always dreamed of living. These are obvious opportunities that you can't miss, because they are delivered to you in neon lights.

For example, Michelle had been in a long-distance relationship with the man she loved for nearly three years. She lived in Florida and he lived in Ohio, and it was impossible for either one of them to move because of their respective jobs. When Michelle's company offered her a transfer to Cleveland, I jokingly asked her if she was going to accept the offer.

"Are you crazy?" she nearly hollered. "This is the miracle I have been waiting for!" For Michelle, this was one of those neon-lit opportunities that she wouldn't dream of passing up.

The second type of opportunity is not obvious and requires that you look beneath the surface. These are the ones you need to root around a bit to find. For instance, when your company merges with another and new positions are available. Perhaps you hear in passing that a business you are interested in is opening a branch office in a city close to your home. Maybe someone tells you about a hot initial public offering and you are invited to invest. A friend invites you to go whitewater rafting on a river you have never seen. These opportunities require a little more exploration and excavation. These are the ones that make you say "Hmm. Maybe . . ."

The universe is constantly in flux. Change is a constant. Changes can occur in your private life or far away on the front page of the newspaper. With every change that occurs around you, an opportunity is presented. Usually it is buried beneath the surface, but if you are willing, you can excavate it.

Dave worked as an editor at a feature magazine. He liked what he did but wished he had more time to pursue his primary love, which was writing. One afternoon his boss called him into his office and handed him a story about a local true-crime case with some fascinating twists and turns and asked him to research it. Dave took the story back to his desk and was immediately engrossed. As he worked on the story, he kept getting a needling feeling that this was a doorway to some sort of opportunity for him.

Dave didn't sleep a wink that night. He tossed and turned as he wrestled with his thoughts. In the morning, as he was brushing his teeth, the message came through to him loud and clear: He wanted to contact the people involved in the story and write a book about it. It was an incredible tale, and he knew he could do an excellent job with a book. He knew he had the talent to do this, and since he kept up with true-crime books, he was fairly certain that it would be a market-able project.

Dave went to his boss the next day and told him of his plans. His boss supported the decision, although it would mean Dave would have to take an unpaid leave of absence. Within three months, Dave found a publisher for the book and is now spending all his time doing what he loves to do: writing.

This was one of those opportunities that did not come delivered on a silver platter. No one said to Dave, "Would you like to write a book about this story?" nor did anyone hold up a sign that said "You should write a book about this." It took a willingness on Dave's part to peer beneath the surface of his everyday life and find an opportunity amid the daily events.

OPENING YOUR EYES

If your eyes and ears are open, you will see the windows of opportunity open around you. Sometimes they show up as signs, like an ad for a meditation retreat you were deciding whether to attend appearing on the side of your tea box or an acquaintance mentioning a piece of coincidental news to you in passing. The key to noticing opportunities is to have your antennae turned on and be actively looking for them. When you invite opportunities into your life, the universe will cooperate and present various options to you. If you don't see them, you either have closed off your peripheral vision with blinders, or you are so focused on what's in front of you that you miss the obvious.

You need to be awake in order to see opportunities. They are there, waiting for you to become aware of them. You can ignore or overlook them, but either way, they exist. They may not look like what you expected, they might not be the exact ones you hoped for, but like oxygen molecules, *they are still present.*

Try this exercise: Make a list of all the opportunities that were presented to you in the past day. Leave nothing out, including the opportunity to try some exotic sushi for the first time, to go to the movies with your spouse, to try a boxing class at your gym, to take home a stray dog you see on the street, or to buy a certain stock. You probably will be surprised to note how many opportunities come your way in a single day without you even realizing it.

Now spend the next few days seeking out every opportunity that comes your way. For one day, carry a notebook around with you and jot them down. Try to notice every option that is presented to you to expand your horizons, or to learn or experience something new. This does not mean you need to take advantage of every one. The activity is merely a wake-up call to yourself, so that you can be attuned to all the possibilities that surround you.

Every Opportunity Presents a Choice

Some things arrive in their own mysterious hour, on their own terms and not yours, to be seized or relinquished forever. — GAIL GODWIN

The moment that an opportunity presents itself to you, you engage in an immediate assessment process. *Should I? . . . Could I? . . . Do I want this? . . . Do I dare? . . . What if? . . .* All these questions begin swirling around in your head. You need to undertake an internal dialogue—a weighing process—to determine the right course of action for you.

The Assessment Process

The assessment process occurs in three places: your head, your heart, and your gut. When these three zones have fully computed the data and then merge their findings with the other two, you have your choice.

Although you may react initially from the emotional realm or the rational domain, it is a good idea to check in with all the different facets of yourself so that you make an integrated choice. Making just an intellectual decision does not take into consideration your feelings about the situation. Reacting emotionally doesn't integrate your rational and reasonable side. It is only when you consider your thoughts, feelings, hopes, fears, concerns, and ideal outcomes that you can assess an opportunity fully and determine if it is right for you.

Your mind's job is to feed back to you all the data you have collected regarding this specific situation. It will analyze in a rational manner whether this opportunity is a good option for you to take. Try to be as honest and objective as you can, understanding that your mind doesn't have ultimate veto power.

If you have difficulty making decisions about new options, writing out all the notions that are inside really helps clarify your priorities. When you write, simply spill out everything your mind has to say, ideally in lists of pros and cons. As a guideline, try to include the following:

- These people are invested in me taking this action:
- These people will be pleased if I turn it down:
- This opportunity will affect my finances in these ways:
- This opportunity will affect my intellect in these ways:
- This opportunity will affect my emotions in these ways:
- This opportunity will affect my health in these ways:
- This opportunity will affect my career in these ways:
- This opportunity will affect my relationship in these ways:
- The benefits of taking this opportunity might be:
- The risks of taking this opportunity might be:
- The worst-case scenario looks like:
- The best-case scenario looks like:

The purpose of this exercise is to get the thoughts out of your head and on to paper, where they can be addressed one by one. Thoughts trapped inside your head can create a mental prism or hall of mirrors, in which everything looks distorted, bigger, caricatured, and more convoluted than it may be in reality.

The next step is to explore your emotions. After the initial reaction, get an accurate read on how you feel about this new opportunity. Imagine yourself in your new situation and see what feelings it evokes. Do you feel energized, depleted, overwhelmed, excited, silly, or powerful?

Pay attention to your physical reactions. Does your breath catch when you think about it? Do your shoulders slowly climb toward your ears when you envision yourself in this new reality? Do you get butterflies in your stomach or a throbbing sensation in your temples? Does it make you feel lighter, almost lofty? Do you feel overwhelming responsibility or burden? All these are clues into how you really feel.

Again, write all these observations down on paper. This act won't completely clear your psyche of the emotions, but it will allow you to move forward and take the next step. If you are caught up in the emotions of the situation, your ability to make a clear choice is hindered.

Once you have completed the first two steps, you may set aside your mental and emotional processes and listen for your internal gut response. You can access your gut only when you are calm, quiet, and centered within yourself. Your gut is that authentic place inside that says "yes" or "no." Neither emotions nor logic temper it. It is clear, certain, and absolute. In my Inner Negotiation Workshop, we call this gut-level re-sponse a "message." It is similar to those moments when you realize in hindsight that your initial intuition was accurate. You suddenly realize that you knew at the time exactly what you needed to do and, for some strange reason, you didn't trust yourself. Since you didn't trust yourself, you took no ac-tion. You, therefore, see it as a missed opportunity. You might say, "I knew it—I knew it at the time. Why didn't I do what I knew was right?"

The reason that you didn't listen to your gut is either be-cause it was unreasonable or it required you taking a risk. This is precisely what causes people to move into "I don't know."

What if the answer is "I don't know"?

You may not like the answer that surfaces. Often that is the case, which causes people to slide into "I don't know." If you don't like the answer that arises, you might bury it without even realizing it and become caught in a false state of uncer-tainty.

If the answer that surfaces is "I don't know," remember that "I don't know" is a safe response. It is the one that ensures you will not have to face your underlying fears. The haze of "I don't know" can be frustrating, because it means that you can and probably will do nothing. You cannot act, and therefore you are paralyzed.

"I don't know" is a dead end. There is nowhere to go from there; in order to get unstuck, you need to reverse back into knowingness. You will dispel the haze of uncertainty when you are willing to hear your internal response, no matter how uncomfortable or challenging it might be.

How is this done?

When you reinstate your trust in yourself, when you revisit the source of your self-doubt, you essentially open up your intuitive canals and allow the right choice to come to the foreground. Revisit the place inside you that is confident and knows you can handle whatever it is, the place that believes in your abilities and that trusts your instincts. When you operate from that source, "I don't know" vaporizes.

The child in you always knows. It is the adult veneer that gets caught in the sticky web of doubts, fears, and hesitations that constitute uncertainty. I was once out on a hot day with my friend Donna when we passed an ice cream truck. I turned to her and asked if she wanted to get some. Immediately, uncertainty took over, and she said, "Sure. Actually, no. I mean . . . umm . . ."

I laughed, mostly because she looked so endearing as she struggled with her decision about whether to indulge herself with a treat. "What's going on in there?" I asked, tapping the side of her head.

"Well, it's hot, and I would love ice cream, but it's so fattening," she said. "I need to fit into my black dress next weekend. But on the other hand, a little enjoyment won't kill me!"

Donna was clearly stuck in "I don't know," so I did what I always do whenever a client does the same thing. I overrode the not-knowingness and said, "If you *did* know what you wanted here, what would it be?"

"I'd get a vanilla cone with colored sprinkles!" she said, marching up to the ice cream truck and handing the young man her money.

Sometimes you need to banish the adult part of yourself

for a short time in order to get the source of your decision-making ability. Remember, kids always know what they want. Find the child in you and you'll find your answer.

Of course, there may be adult considerations to take into account once you know what you want, but you can deal with those after you know what they are. When you get caught up in those factors before you go to the source, it is difficult to pierce the veil of uncertainty and operate from a place of "I know."

Creative solutions

Sometimes the answer is not black and white, yes or no, here or there. Sometimes it falls into the shades of gray in between, and you will need to come up with a creative solution.

Take, for example, Miranda's story. Miranda came to me in a state bordering on agony. She had been wrestling with whether to leave her life as a stay-at-home mom and take a job that had been offered to her.

I asked her how she felt about the job and she replied, "Excited." I asked her about her concerns and she told me this: "I love being a mother. I love knowing that I can make a difference in one person's life by loving her and being there for her. It is important for me to see the direct effects of my care and attention. If I take this job, I am afraid that I will cheat my daughter, that I will get wrapped up in the corporate world, the deadlines, the politics, become stressed, become overcommitted and feel guilty that I can't win at home or at work."

I asked Miranda what she wanted. She said, "That's the problem, I don't know. All the options look appealing but a little scary. I don't know if I can handle the responsibilities in both places. In addition, I'm not sure I want to hand my daughter over to child care everyday."

I then asked her the pivotal question that leads to creative solutions: What would it take to make all this work? How would she set up her life if she were totally in charge? This question opens you up to the possibility that you can have everything you want, if you are willing to create it. There is always a way.

Her response was interesting. "I would work part time from home and part time in the office. My hours would be flexible and I could have boundaries that were respected. I would be able to be a stay-at-home mother, have additional support from someone, and be able to stay in the mainstream of work without it totally devouring my life."

I looked at her lucid expression and commented, "It sounds to me as if you really do know what you want. That is crystal clear."

She turned to me astonished at her own clarity and said, "I guess I do know, but perhaps I don't believe it's possible. I don't know that anyone at that firm would agree to my terms." I let her know that knowing what you want is the first step in the process; believing it is possible is the second. Making it happen is the third and so on.

Miranda is a clear example of someone who is caught in the web of spaghetti in her mind. Picture a large pot of spaghetti with all the noodles entangled. Each noodle represents a thought, concern, reservation, feeling, fear, or consideration. All of them are entangled. Through gentle questioning,

Miranda could begin to see the individual strands separated into individual issues. This process that I do and teach serves as a catalyst to create mental clarity. In a very short time, Miranda shifted from "I don't know what I want" to "I know exactly what I want." When she reached this stage, she hadn't manifested her wish, but she had completed the first step in the process successfully.

The process of moving from "I don't know what I want" to "I have everything I dreamed of" has five distinct steps:

Step one: "I don't know what I want and I can't be it, do it, or have it."

Step two: "I know what I want, but I can't have it."

Step three: "I know what I want and I can have some of it."

Step four: "I know what I want and I can have it all."

Step five: "I have what I want."

These steps form what resembles a vertical staircase progression. You start at the bottom step, and each step takes you closer to your ideal life. Through creative solutions, you move from one step to the next until you have what it is that you want.

You may be on different steps with each different issue in your life. Perhaps you are on the top step with your relationship with your body, at the bottom step with your career, and on the middle step with your romantic relationship. If you can see where you are on the staircase, you can determine what is necessary to move to the next step.

Before you can progress anywhere on this staircase, how-ever, you will need to tackle the first step of moving out of "I don't know." If necessary, ask yourself one of the three piv-otal questions:

1. What would you do if you *did* know?
2. How would you proceed if you were totally in charge of the situation?
3. If you were free of expectations, financial con-straints, time factors, and responsibilities, what would you do?

The answers to these questions might be what makes you "pop"—in other words, what removes the clouds from your clear vision and opens you to the realm of creative solutions. Be open to any and all possibilities that surface. You don't nec-essarily need to act on any of the creative solutions you come up with, but don't discard them before you give yourself a chance to consider them.

THE TIMING FACTOR

Sometimes opportunities will need to pass because the timing is off. What is being presented to you may overload you, un-balance you, cause you too much stress, create too many rela-tionships to manage. Perhaps you simply have too many plates in the air, or financing is stretched to the limit, or you haven't found the right people in order to delegate. Or perhaps the opportunity just came along too late, or before you were ready for it.

Avery was an assistant to a powerful talent agent. His goal was to get promoted to an agent himself one day, when he had learned all that he needed to from his boss and mentor.

Approximately six months after he was hired, Avery arrived at work and saw his boss packing boxes. When he asked what had happened, his boss told him that he had just been let go. "Be prepared," his mentor told him. "They will probably offer you my job. That's the way it works around here."

Sure enough, they did. The powers-that-be decided that Avery was the one to take over his boss's sizable client list and assume the responsibility of finding the client-actors work. At first, Avery was excited about the possibility. Being an agent meant making a lot of money, going to lunch with powerful movie and television executives, and generally hobnobbing with celebrities. It also meant structuring complicated deals, establishing and relying on strong relationships, assessing which roles were worth taking, and knowing how to handle the demanding and sometimes high-maintenance clients. In the majority of these areas Avery was a neophyte.

In his heart, Avery knew he was not ready for this opportunity. He simply had not learned enough yet to accept such responsibility. He wanted to be an agent, but he wanted more to be a *good* agent—not one in title only. He knew he did not know enough about the business yet, in terms of actual information and nuance, to serve the clients well. In turn, he knew that that ultimately meant it wouldn't be long before he, too, was packing his things. He turned down the job offer, knowing that it was the right opportunity but the wrong time for him.

Marlene's situation was somewhat different. She was a pediatrician in a large hospital who had made the decision to go into private practice with two other doctors. Immediately after making this decision, but before she informed her employer, she was offered a promotion to become the head of the entire pediatric ward. This was a tremendous opportunity, and Marlene found herself at a crossroads.

When the thrill of being offered such a major position wore off, Marlene remembered the reason why she had originally decided to leave the hospital setting: politics. She was tired of having to deal with so much bureaucracy in order to practice medicine. She turned the promotion down and continued with her plans. The opportunity came along just a little too late.

Much of life is about timing. We find our beloved when both people are ready, we find the right job when the universe lines up our talents and an employer's need, and we find the right situation when we are ready for it. If an opportunity comes your way at the wrong time, let it pass.

You'll know when the time is right to seize the next one.

THE COST FACTOR

Sometimes what you have to give up is greater than what you would gain if you took the opportunity. As you go through the assessment process, you will need to do a cost/benefit analysis to establish whether the opportunity presented is one that will pay off for you or one whose price will be too great to justify taking.

To do such an analysis, take into account what the cost will be to your time, your career path, your relationship, your private time, your family life, and your mental, emotional, physical, and spiritual health. If the results that come up indicate that taking this opportunity will stretch you too tight or too thin, then you will have to take this into account when you make your choice.

Eleanor was an industrial psychologist who had been working in a private consulting firm for several years when she was offered a position as the on-staff counselor to a major national real estate company. This was an exciting opportunity for her, although taking it meant making some serious life adjustments. The hours would be long, she would be required to travel 70 percent of the time, and she would have to be available for seminars for two out of the four weekends a month. After discussing it with her husband, who agreed he would take over the daily care of their two grade-school children, Eleanor decided this was a terrific career opportunity, and she took the job.

The work was interesting and fulfilling but also highly demanding. Within three months, Eleanor was exhausted. She often arrived home after 11:00 P.M., gobbled leftovers, and fell into bed without spending any quality time with her family. As a result, she gained weight and looked and felt drained. She grew more and more irritable with each passing day, until she finally realized that the job was putting too much of a strain on her family life, not to mention her physical health. The cost outweighed the benefits, and she resigned. She returned to her original position, which had flexible hours and allowed her to decide how much time she spent on the road.

About a year later, Eleanor was again offered a lucrative position, this time at a high-profile brokerage firm. Again, the hours would be long, and considerable travel was required. It took Eleanor less than a day to assess the cost/benefit analysis, and learning from her past experience, she turned down the position. She wanted to preserve the time she had with her family now and decided that she would consider a position like that in the future, perhaps when her children left for college.

Opportunities that cost you more than you have to give are just not worth it. If your cost/benefit analysis reveals that you will need to give up more than you will get in return, release the opportunity to the universe. It simply wasn't the right one for you.

When You Have Made Your Choice

The moment you make your choice, write down what you have chosen, make sure you date it, and tell your core group or inner circle what you have chosen. Doing this is important because it sets up external accountability that will help keep you on track. People often do this when they are trying to modify their behavior in some way, such as quitting smoking or eliminating procrastination. One of the reasons the personal coaching field is so explosive is because people require external accountability. If you are required to check in and let someone know that you did what you said, then you are less likely to let yourself off the hook. Think of New Year's resolutions: The reason they usually fall by the wayside around March 1 is because of a lack of external accountability.

Every choice requires you to stretch out of your comfort zone. It requires you to take a risk, which, by definition, is unsettling. As soon as your mind starts to consider what you are about to do, it will produce all of the data to reverse your choice. You have heard people say "I changed my mind." "I talked to people I know and they think it's too risky." "I need to stay with the stable job that I've been doing for years." In sales, this is called buyer's remorse; however, in personal motivation we call it the "yeah buts" taking over and gobbling up the choices.

When you know what you want, and you feel the sizzle of excitement, write it, tell your closest support network, and commit to going for it. Move into doing and out of thinking about it.

Do not hesitate.

Do not waffle.

Do not wait.

Do not give yourself any opportunity to renege on your choice. When you have chosen from your authentic self, all your defenses—your ego, your inner critic, your fears—will rise up like a battalion and do everything they can to hold you back.

The negaholics around you will assist you in arguing for your limitations. Although your inner resolve may be strong, why test it against the combined forces of your doubts and everyone else's projected limits?

Venturing into the Unknown

And the trouble is, if you don't risk anything, you risk even more.

—Erica Jong

Seizing opportunities leads you into the vast unknown. Choosing something new can be unsettling, but it also can be one of the most exhilarating feelings in life.

When I was in my early twenties and still acting, I was offered the chance to go to New York and perform in *As You Like It* in Shakespeare in the Park. Doing Shakespeare in the Park had been a dream of mine for years. However, since I had traded acting for another passion, I had tucked that dream in the I-guess-it-will-never-happen file. Needless to say, I was thrilled at the prospect of making this unfulfilled dream come true.

Being in that play at that point meant temporarily leaving graduate school, my home in Minnesota, and my husband of six months, and going to New York by myself. This had been my lifelong dream, and although rationally it seemed as if I were crazy and shouldn't go, my gut told me I needed to do this. I knew I couldn't live my life knowing that I had passed up such an opportunity.

I packed my bags, flew to New York, got up on that stage, and did what I loved to do one last time. It was, of course, one of the best summers of my life. With no guarantees, no promises, no handrails to hold on to, I trusted my gut so totally that I was living a natural high every day.

Recently, someone sent me slides of photos from that

summer. There is a series of pictures of me in costume, standing under a tree in Central Park, and my face is beaming. I am absolutely glowing with happiness. When I showed that photo to a young friend of mine, she asked me to make a copy so she could display it on her desk as a reminder that taking risks is one of the surest ways to invite joy into your life.

Taking Risks

Taking a risk means that you stretch out of your comfort zone and do something that has no guarantee attached. It means that you listen to the sizzle, pay attention to the internal bubbles of excitement, and honor the light in your eyes. It means that you do something that is not logical, rational, or reasonable but rather intuitive. It means going against conventional wisdom and really listening to the singing of your heart. Taking a risk is not foolhardy, but it isn't necessarily always sensible, either. It usually lies somewhere in between.

Taking a risk requires both self-trust and the willingness to make a mistake. Whether all of your hopes and expectations become fulfilled or not, there will be a plethora of things to learn from the experience.

How do you know when to take the risk? When the pull of the thrill is as powerful as a magnet; when it has you in its grasp and won't let go; when you are ready and willing to accept whatever comes your way as a result. That is when you know it is time to take the leap.

Between the secure world in which you have planted yourself and the new life that you want to create is a chasm. It is up to you to build the initial bridge between those two worlds. The challenge arises after you have done your due diligence.

That is when you realize that after all you have already done—all the thinking, researching, assessing, and deciding—you can't really know anything until you have put yourself in the experience.

The last inch or mile is the unknowable zone. You can know the answer only by leaving what you know and going for it. This is where it feels like leaping into the void. Once you lift the first foot to move it forward, the trailing foot must leave the ground before your first foot makes solid contact. This "ungrounded" feeling is the risk-taking moment. With nothing under you and nothing to hold on to, you must trust yourself absolutely. The feeling is closest one can come to emotional flight.

Nike says: "Just do it!" Of course, this is easier said than done, but there is a point at which that is all that is left to do. After you satisfy your need for information and knowledge, answer all the questions in your mind, ask everyone you know for an opinion, look it up on the Internet, read everything you can get your hands on, it's time to either go for it or not. If you decide the opportunity is not for you, then you turn it down. If you decide you want to go for it, then you must venture into the unknown and take the risk.

Are you ready to leap?

Watch Out for Bunny Trails

The road to success has many tempting parking places.

— Steve Potter

Sometimes what looks like a shimmering path turns out to be a bunny trail leading nowhere except down a rabbit hole. A bunny trail is a short-term detour that takes you off course. It is a distraction that may look enticing when it first appears but ultimately turns you further from where you wanted to go. The divergence from your path acts as an interruption, which usually costs you valuable time, effort, perhaps money, and other resources.

A bunny trail is not an opportunity that you took that did not work out as you had planned. Nor is a bunny trail an opportunity you passed up. Rather, a bunny trail is a detour you consciously choose. It is a variance from your path from which you can learn lessons.

Detours Along the Way

Why do people choose detours? Sometimes it is out of self-sabotage, sometimes it is because they believe they have found a shortcut to success, and sometimes it is just for the sheer enjoyment of what the bunny trail promises at its end. Whatever the reason, detours happen frequently, usually more than once to the same person. The best you can do is pay attention and watch out for them; you also can learn from the experience as you look up from the rabbit hole.

Let's say your goal is to find a partner and get married. You establish this as your goal, figure out the action steps you are going to take to find this person, and go out into the world with your mission. Then someone comes along whom you know you would never marry because he or she is just not right for you, but you find yourself attracted to this person and hence end up in a casual relationship.

If experimenting with different dating partners was your goal, then you would be on track. But since your original goal was to find a marriage partner, you have gone down a bunny trail. The champagne and nights out dancing may be entertaining and fun, but in the end, you will need to take the time and effort to find your way back to your original course in order to succeed at your goal.

I am certainly not arguing against having fun. In fact, I am a great advocate of fun. The greatest fun is the realization of your ultimate dreams. If you have your heart set on a goal that you know will make you happy, settling for crumbs that take you hither and yon and prevent you from grabbing the brass ring aren't worth it in the end.

Howard was a venture capitalist who specialized in real estate investments. He had a vision of building and owning a small inn on a Caribbean island where he and his wife eventually could retire. This would take considerable capital, not to mention a lot of hard work. But Howard was up to the challenges.

The problem was that Howard could never say no to any other good real estate opportunities that came his way. One year it was a parking garage in Manhattan, the next it was an office building in New Jersey. Each of these ventures required large investments of his money that he had earmarked for the inn. They also consumed a great deal of his time and energy, which he needed to research island properties.

Nor could Howard say "no" to any offers that looked like fun, such as traveling to Scotland with his three golfing partners to play the famed St. Andrews course. Opportunities like these were what Howard deemed "once in a lifetime." However, with every piece of property Howard bought and every trip he spent valuable time and money on, he drove himself further and further from those sandy beaches of the Caribbean.

RECOGNIZING BUNNY TRAILS

How do you recognize bunny trails? There are three ways. First, they all generally have one thing in common: They look *very* enticing. They are the cotton candy of opportunities: fluffy and brightly colored. Yet just like that sugary confection on your tongue, they melt away and leave you quite unsatisfied.

Second, they focus on the short term rather than the long term. They offer instant gratification and immediate payoff but lack long-term satisfaction and fulfillment. When we toss aside our long-term plans for immediate gratification—however temporary it may be—we are following a bunny trail.

Third, they usually arouse defensiveness in those who follow them. They invite you to throw caution to the wind and force you to defend your actions to those who call you on your choices. If you find yourself overly defensive about why you are following a certain path (e.g., "I *need* this," "I *won't* feel guilty about it!), there is a good chance you are headed in the direction of a rabbit hole.

What I am referring to is not sacrifice; it is commitment. Sometimes you will be called upon to say "no" to something you desire right now in order to achieve something you desire more later on. It can be a sacrifice if you focus on what you are giving up, but it is a commitment if you focus on your ability to remain dedicated to your most precious visions. It all depends on how you look at it.

For example, if your goal is to lose ten pounds, you can look at passing up a piece of chocolate cake as a sacrifice, or you can look at it as a reinforcement of your commitment to your desired outcome. If you view it as the former, you will feel deprived. If you view it as the latter, however, the self-affirmation you experience will feel just as delicious as that slice of cake.

The bottom line is this: Bunny trails lead to short-term gratification, and real opportunities are chances to succeed at your long-term goals. Depending on which is more important to you, you can either experience a small taste of delight or hold out for the whole gourmet meal. The choice is yours.

During the course of everyday life, opportunities are constantly presented in various forms. If you are paying attention, you will notice them. If you listen to your gut, trust yourself, and don't get distracted by bunny trails, you can choose the opportunities that will lead you to the fulfillment of your goals and your life path.

Know this: Opportunities are always out there. The question is: Are you recognizing the ones for you?

Rule Seven

Each Setback Provides Valuable Lessons

*There will be disappointments and perceived failures
along the way. Learning from these experiences offers
you precious insight that can lead to future successes.*

uccess and failure are as intricately entwined as the
moon and the tide, the mountains and the valleys,
and the sunshine and the rain. Just as nature provides
a sense of balance in the natural world, the universe provides
equilibrium in the human realm through the experiences of
highs and lows.

There is sound reason behind the adage that claims you
cannot know the sweetness of success unless you have tasted
the bitterness of failure. You cannot fully appreciate the joy of
fulfillment unless you have traveled through the eye of adver-

sity, been seriously defeated by setbacks, or had the crushing wave of disappointment knock you down so that you actually considered not getting up again.

Nearly every person who has ever succeeded has experienced setbacks. Perhaps they witnessed their dreams shattered, their aspirations scorned and ridiculed, or their goals dashed against the bricks of financial institutions. They have had to deal with frustration, rejection, and disappointment and learn ways to rebound from their setbacks.

Most of us would prefer an obstacle-free, totally supportive, no-limit life. Who would not rather succeed brilliantly each and every time? But, as most of us are all too aware, life is simply not like that. There are hurdles to cross, roadblocks around which to maneuver, and, at times, setbacks from which to recover.

There will be times as you travel your path that you encounter obstacles. As you make your way, there is always the potential that you will fall, scrape your knees, and perhaps even career off the embankment. Most likely you will experience moments that look like failure, that feel too overwhelming to face.

The challenge in those moments is to tap your source of determination so that you can pick yourself up, dust off the grit of embarrassment, wounded pride, or shaken confidence, and move forward. Of course, you will need to take the time to process your experience first, so that you may heal properly, and so that you can gain perspective and learn from what happened.

If you are going to succeed in life and consequently be fulfilled, then you must face the disappointments and failures that life deals you and discover the value inherent in them. No one likes disappointments, and no one likes to miss their mark. The wise ones, however, are not the ones who never falter. They are the ones who do and who use those setbacks as opportunities to grow so that they may venture forward toward future success.

WHEN SETBACKS OCCUR: GIVING UP VERSUS MOVING FORWARD

I am not discouraged, because every wrong attempt discarded is another step forward. —THOMAS EDISON

When disappointments occur, you are immediately faced with a choice. You have one of two options. You can fall down and stay down, weighted by self-recrimination and an attitude of defeat. Or you can process the disappointment, persevere in your efforts either by returning to your path or by charting a revised one, and eventually learn and grow from what happened. In other words, you can either give up or move forward.

AN ATTITUDE OF DEFEAT

The first option is the one you will mostly likely be drawn to immediately following a setback. Just as with grief, the first stage after a perceived failure is usually denial. It hurts to see your dreams shattered and your efforts go down the drain, so it is natural that your first instinct would be to hide, to pull life's covers over your head and give up on yourself and your chances to get where you wanted to go. The problem comes when you stay under the covers and refuse to come out after the initial shock has worn off.

Daniel was an example of this scenario. It was Daniel's dream to attend Harvard University. He had wanted to wear that crimson and gold insignia for as long as he could remember. He studied hard in high school, participated in many extracurricular activities, and did all that he could to make himself attractive to the college board. Unfortunately, however, Daniel's scores on the SAT's were not quite high enough to meet Harvard's standards, and his application was denied.

Daniel was devastated. He had always possessed a fragile sense of self-esteem, and hence he took this rejection quite hard. When he received the thin envelope bearing the bad news in the mail, he went straight up to his room and remained there for the remainder of the evening. Although his parents tried to console him over the next few weeks by reminding him that there were plenty of other colleges to which he could apply and surely be accepted, Daniel responded with disinterest. He did nothing to help himself in the following months, and much to his parents' unhappiness, one day he announced that he was not going to go to college at all. Apparently, he had taken the rejection from Harvard so hard that his self-confidence was too shredded to withstand any further efforts.

Thankfully, Daniel's parents were smart enough to recognize that their son was suffering from a depression over the disappointment and arranged for him to see a qualified therapist. It took a while, but eventually Daniel regained his intellectual confidence and began to peek out from under the covers. The following spring he came to see me, and together we strategized a new plan. He sent out applications to several top schools and was accepted at Duke University.

There are also those who unconsciously choose defeat and become angry, maybe even bitter. This is the it's-not-fair approach to coping with a setback. This course of action leads to the proverbial chip on your shoulder. Have you ever known people who carry around a past failure with them like a badge? They flash it often, usually when life feels challenging. The loss, disappointment, or setback they experienced becomes a reason for them to be angry at the world. They resent the lot they have drawn and believe fate is against them. Causality is not part of their reality.

Marsha was such a case. At forty-five, Marsha was an executive at a telecommunications company. She had been working toward being named chief operating officer for years, and when the person in that position retired, she and everyone else were certain that Marsha would be promoted. However, management chose instead to bring in a younger person from the outside—to, as they put it, "infuse new energy in the company."

Marsha did not accept the news gracefully. Of course she was disappointed, and probably she should have taken this as a signal either to look at other opportunities or to reassess her future, but instead, she focused all her energy on being angry and resentful. She began slacking off at work, missing important meetings, and generally walking around the office with a scowl on her face. She disparaged her new boss and generally put a damper not only on the morale of everyone around her but also on her future prospects at the company. She remained stuck in her resentment and hence frozen in her career.

I lost track of Marsha after she came to see me and refused to recognize how her own bitterness was directly in her way. She could not break through the wall of hostility that she built around her and bore her victimization as the sole and central cause of blame in her life. I don't know if she finally discovered that all she needed to do to reinstate herself on the path to success was process the disappointment, release the anger, and plan a way to move forward.

CHOOSING TO RECOVER

The latter option is obviously the optimal one. Certainly you will experience feelings of defeat, like Daniel, or anger, like Marsha. The bouncing-back option is the one in which you deal with these emotions, feel whatever comes up, process what happened, and then put the experience in perspective and choose to move forward. Recovery occurs when you weave setbacks into your personal history rather than allowing them to be the end of your story.

Dwelling on setbacks keeps you stalled in nowhere land. There is a wonderful Mary Engelbreit cartoon titled "Don't Look Back" that shows a fork in the road; one sign points to "your life," and the other points to a place called "no longer an option." If you continue to focus on what could have been rather than on what is, you are denying your current reality. How can you expect ever to move forward if you are trapped in the past?

Setbacks are what build character. They are what separate the lucky from the truly successful. It is not the person who wins the first time out of the gate who demonstrates strength, stamina, wisdom, and grit. Rather, it is the one who has run before and narrowly missed the finish line—who runs with all he or she is worth. Such people are the ones for whom victory tastes the sweetest.

It all comes down to how you perceive your experience. You can view it as a failure, which evokes images and feelings of devastation and dead ends. The other option is to view it as a setback, which is more of a temporary impediment on your path. Both bring up powerful emotions; however, the real difference between the two is how you frame your experience in the context of your future. Will this be the end of the road or just a deterrent on your path to future success?

PERSEVERANCE: THE PATH OF THE DETERMINED

Never, never, never quit.

—WINSTON CHURCHILL

Determination is the state of being mentally committed to an outcome, when you are determined you will do whatever it takes to achieve your objective. Determined people do not let obstacles bar their path but rather find some way to remove the boulders or barriers and make seemingly impossible things happen. If you are determined, giving up is not an option. You persevere no matter what.

Ruby and Neil were a married couple in their twenties from Texas who wanted to become parents. Their goal was to get pregnant by the end of the year, but it was not to be. After trying to conceive through regular means for close to a year, they tried fertility drugs. Although the drugs were costly and caused a considerable drain on their savings, they wanted a child more than they wanted money stored in the bank. After several months they were told that the fertility drugs were not working and that they would need to try in vitro fertilization, another costly procedure. They did, with unfortunately no results, due to a rare genetic condition they discovered through extensive blood tests. Eventually, their doctor suggested that they consider adoption alternatives, since their chances of conceiving were so slim.

At that point, Ruby and Neil obviously experienced a surge of tough emotions. They were sad, angry, frustrated, and disappointed. They felt cheated as they looked around and saw so many people their age who were able to conceive. Ruby actually found herself in the supermarket one day with tears streaming down her face when she stood behind a young mother with her baby strapped to her back. They did not indulge themselves, however, in discouragement. They wanted to be parents so badly that they refused to give up. They knew there had to be a way, and they were determined to find it.

"Finding a way" became their all-consuming project. They researched fertility specialists around the country and got a second opinion. When the first doctor's findings were confirmed, they turned their efforts toward learning about surrogate mothers. They combed the Internet, read everything they could find, and interviewed people who had gone that route. Ultimately they decided that option was not for them, so they set about finding a child to adopt. They registered with agencies and orphanages around the country until they were matched up with a young pregnant woman in Seattle who knew she planned to give her baby up for adoption at birth.

One year and six months later, Ruby and Neil were on a plane, on their way to Seattle for the birth of their daughter. Through sheer perseverance, they made their deepest wish a reality, as they are now parents to a beautiful baby girl. It took considerable time, energy, and resources, but they persevered in their efforts. Frustration might have caused them to give up anywhere along the way had they not been so determined.

Determined people create new footprints in the snow. When they are told "things will never work," they merely take it in stride and move on to the next opportunity. This is not to say they never feel down, lose faith, or have second thoughts. That is all part of the human experience.

What "Determination" Looks Like

The difference between average and successful people is that successful people do not waste time arguing for their limitations, they transcend them. They take their fair share of lumps and continue on regardless. Although bruised and sometimes emotionally injured, they pick themselves up and start over again. Like those blow-up clown punching bags, they refuse to stay down.

Ruby and Neil could have given up. They could have said the search was too hard, too time-consuming, or too costly. They could have become mired in self-pity and allowed the setback to destroy their marriage. Instead, they chose determination over defeat.

Those who are determined interpret roadblocks as detour

signs rather than dead ends. They always look for another way to get where they want to go, even if it was not the original route they had mapped out.

Successful people also create a support network of people who don't "believe" them if and when they argue for their limitations. No matter how convincing they are to their inner circle, previously they have made it abundantly clear that these moments of doubt are not to be taken seriously. Those around them know and remind them that they have enough determination to sustain them, even in those moments when that quality is hard to recall.

Determination is what John F. Kennedy embodied in 1961 when he said we would put a man on the moon before the end of the decade.

Determination is the force that drove Walt Disney to persevere in building his dream, despite having to declare bankruptcy five times.

Determination is what drove Michael Jordan to keep practicing and improving his game after he was cut from his high school basketball team.

Best-selling author John Grisham, who has 80 million books in print worldwide, was surely fueled by determination after thirty-five publishers originally turned down his work.

Examples such as these are what you can draw on in those moments when you think that perhaps you are ready to give up, cave in, or abandon your dream. I know I have needed to use the determination of others for inspiration when I feel the gravity vortex pulling me down and things seem too difficult.

Many years ago my organization experienced a major setback. By 1979 we had been very successful, doubling every year for five years in revenues, programs, and staff. People actually said I had a magic touch, observing that anything I touched turned to gold. We were growing, clients were turning dreams into reality, and the road ahead looked crystal clear. We had leased a 10,000-square-foot building in San Francisco to house our corporate offices as well as three seminar rooms. The plan was airtight—or so we thought. The design was beautiful, clients were plentiful, and the path ahead looked optimistic.

After we had spent $300,000 on the design and construction of the interior, we discovered to our dismay that we couldn't conduct more than one seminar at a time. The sound engineer hadn't taken our word seriously that people need to be able to fully express themselves in our programs, and the noise bleed between rooms was unacceptable. All of our projections became invalid, since all the numbers were diminished by 66 percent. It was a disaster.

We were devastated. This was everything we had worked for and dreamed about, and now, because of one error, it was all going up in smoke. Part of me felt defeated, as if the size and scope of the problem was too big to overcome. Part of me felt like a little girl, wanting to be rescued. And part of me wanted to take the easiest way and just give up.

Thankfully, a bigger part of me chose to fight to stay afloat. As a management consultant, I had counseled so many other businesspeople who had encountered circumstances of equal difficulty. There was the publishing company that had to make a major unforeseen investment in desktop publishing, the bank that had to shift from its old brick-and-mortar paradigm to consultative sales, and the manufacturing company that had to change its culture to valuing people over their stock price. I had coached and witnessed them through the down times back to the moments of shining glory and achievement. I knew recovery through determination was possible in the abstract; and I knew what I needed to do was apply that abstract possibility to my own reality.

We had a meeting to examine our alternatives. We could sue the designer and the sound engineer. We could beat ourselves up for this costly error. We were advised to declare Chapter 7 and then Chapter 11 bankruptcy and close the business. All options looked grim, but collectively, our determination outweighed our willingness to lose all that we had worked so hard to create.

None of the principals wanted to give up the business, not to mention the fact that we were not litigious people. Taking ourselves to task seemed extremely unproductive, so we kept searching for another alternative. Finally, Barbara, our CPA and partner, had a flash of insight. "We could sublease the building, eliminating the overhead, find a smaller, more reasonable office space, and pay off our debt." It was a long-term plan, but it seemed to achieve our objectives. This plan would allow us to keep the business going while taking responsibility for the mistake and learning our lessons.

We spoke to our creditors and asked if they would work with us, and they agreed. We mapped out a strategic plan involving new projections, profit and losses, paybacks, and a revised schedule of courses. The plan involved doing diligence for many years, but it worked. We subleased the building, secured reasonable office space, paid off all of our creditors, and made it through the crunch. Here we are, twenty-six years later, still offering consulting, workshops, seminars, and training programs for satisfied clients throughout the world.

I can't say the process was easy. There were times when it simply wasn't fun. There were snags in the plan and long stretches without any time off, but eventually, with the commitment of the entire team, it worked. We actually had a bonus occur; the change in marketing strategy caused us to expand first nationally and then, nine years later, internationally. If we hadn't made what looked like an egregious error, we never would have been forced to rethink our master plan. As it turned out, shifting away from massive structures and literally going to the people instead of expecting them to come to us in San Francisco made our business responsive, flexible, and "virtual" before it was ever fashionable.

When have you been dealt a hand that you didn't anticipate? When have you been given a crisis/opportunity that you were certain you didn't choose? When have you risen to the occasion, through your determination, and made the seemingly impossible happen?

Give yourself credit for such action, for it is those experiences that build strong character. Remember those moments and draw on them when you need to, so that you can choose perseverance when life throws setbacks in your way in the future. Others have done it, and so can you.

All it takes is the determination to keep on going.

THE STING OF DISAPPOINTMENT

The shell must break before the bird can fly.

—ALFRED LORD TENNYSON

If you are alive, chances are that at some time or another, you have been tested by disappointments. If you are to succeed, however, you must learn how to deal with disappointments, how to process the feelings involved, and how to overcome setbacks and difficulties.

Even before you begin taking action on your goals, you have to allow room in your consciousness for disappointment. You need to acknowledge the potential of obstacles and the possibility that the outcome might not be exactly as you hoped. This is not to say that you should focus on it; in fact, just the opposite. By bringing the shadow of potential disappointment to light, you diminish its power and make it less threatening. Doing this allows you to get on with the business at hand rather than worrying about the what-ifs. When you admit the worst-case scenario, you don't have to hide from it, since you know it can never catch you by surprise.

The paradox is holding simultaneously the glimmer of possibility and the reality of disillusionment. This fine-edge sword allows you to be fully aware of the potential loss of your goal while simultaneously holding the future possibility of the fulfillment of your dream. In other words, you must let go before you create.

ANTICIPATING SETBACKS

Cheryl was days away from her audition with a renowned modern dance company. She had always dreamed of dancing for this troupe, and for the first time in several years, there were openings for new people to join. She had been studying dance since she was twelve years old and had been practicing diligently every day for the past six months for this audition. Still, she was overcome with panic, so at the advice of a friend, she came to see me.

"What is it exactly that you are so terrified about?" I asked this graceful woman who sat before me, white as a sheet.

"I'm just so afraid that I'll mess up, and then I won't get invited to join the troupe, and then everything I've worked for will be down the drain," she said.

"What is the worst thing that can happen?" I asked.

"I could make a fool of myself in the audition."

"And then what?" I pressed.

"Then I wouldn't get in," she responded.

"And then what?"

"Well, then I'd have to start all over."

"And would you survive?" I asked gently.

Cheryl thought about it for a moment. "Yes, I suppose I would." The moment she said this, she looked relieved. The tension eased from her face, and she smiled for the first time since she walked in the door.

It wasn't until Cheryl was able to follow her fear of being disappointed to its worst-case scenario that she could see how much of a hold this worry had over her. When she saw that even the worst-case scenario didn't mean total emotional destruction and her demise, she was freed from the panic of not succeeding.

You can allow for the possibility of setbacks without necessarily dwelling on them. Anticipating a setback is like anticipating an injury: You can allow room for the possibility yet not become so focused on it that you cause it to happen. Let's imagine that you are skiing. If you focus on the idea that you could fall, there is a good chance you will. Have you ever tried so hard not to fall that that is precisely what you end up doing? If you are aware that you could fall and choose instead to focus on skiing rather than falling, there is a less of a chance of landing on your behind in the snow.

Remember, what you focus on, you get more of. Conversely, what you try to deny always finds a way to resurface. The trick is to acknowledge that setbacks may happen without dwelling on the possibility.

PROCESSING DISAPPOINTMENT

Disappointment is similar to grief. You must be willing to feel the experience of it and not just gloss over it if you hope to recover from it.

Your feelings about unfulfilled expectations must go somewhere. You can suppress those feelings because they are too uncomfortable to deal with or because it is too painful to come to terms with them. If you don't deal with them, however, you probably will have to repeat disappointment, setback, or failure because you bypassed the initial experience. If you don't experience the loss, it can get in your way, as lessons will be repeated until learned.

There are certain steps associated with coping with disappointment. First of all, you need to give yourself time to process what has happened. This processing happens in three different realms: the physical, the psychological, and the emotional.

The physical realm

The first and the fastest part of a setback is the processing of the physical changes, the ones that happen immediately around you. For instance, if you have been laid off, you must pack up your personal possessions and bring closure to all the details surrounding your employment. This may include an exit interview, outplacement, and the like. You will need to tend to the immediate concerns that will arise, such as assessing your financial status, and arranging for health insurance. In other words, you will need to take care of the realistic details and circumstances that arise as a result of the experience.

Let's take another example, such as the loss of a relationship that you had high hopes for. In the physical realm, the first thing you will need to deal with is the division of belongings, then how you will spend your free time without that person.

Focusing on the physical shifts that occur first is important and necessary. Doing this gives you immediate tasks, albeit small ones, to focus your attention on. By taking care of yourself and what must get done, you keep yourself energized and on the game board.

The psychological realm

The second phase of the process is psychological. In this phase you deal with changing mental traffic patterns, how you will be spending your time, and the options and choices that you need to consider. You are addressing what this disappointment or setback really means to you.

For example, if we again take the example of losing your job, you will need to consider who you are after you hand in your old business cards and your security keycard. Since so many people confuse who they are with what they do, you have the task of redefining yourself without your job. Simply put, you must have an answer when people ask "What do you do?" Losing a job can become a self-esteem issue, which is something to process in and of itself.

If the disappointment comes from what you perceive as a personal failure, as happened with a surgeon I once counseled, who was riddled with grief over losing a young patient on the operating table, you will need to examine what the loss means to you and try to put it into some kind of perspective. You will need to understand how the experience fits into the overarching journey of your life.

Many people turn to professionals for assistance with the psychological process. Because I am a motivational coach, many people come to me because they are trying to make sense of a major life setback. Whether it is from a coach, a therapist, or even a good friend, seek input and assistance when you need it. It does not mean you are weak; rather, it means you are wise enough to draw on the insight and support of those around you.

The emotional realm

The third phase of the process is emotional. This phase is the most difficult and, for many people, takes the longest. Packing boxes and handing in your key are more tangible than what you feel about a loss, setback, or disappointment. If you have been doing your job quite well, even with a degree of excellence, and the company you work for was acquired, it makes perfect sense that certain people will have to go. However, that doesn't make it easier emotionally to understand the situation. After all, understanding is psychological, and feelings are emotional.

All too often, people try to rationalize an experience of loss with sound logical explanations. Reason doesn't help because the feelings are irrational. Perhaps you disliked your job and the downsizing is actually good news; then you should be elated. Maybe you are and yet maybe this is the familiar and comfortable work environment that you have come to every day for years, even decades. The loss might be associated with loss of identity by leaving a situation that was less than ideal but was as familiar as home.

Emotions take their toll on even the most astute "thinker." Emotions include sadness, grief, anger, resentment, fear, anxiety, paralysis, depression, and even relief, elation, and excitement. Processing the emotions may take more time than you anticipated. It might be less comfortable than you hoped. It might be less controllable than you imagined. Emotions are the third phase of processing the disappointment, and they must be addressed if you are to move on and put the event in your past.

Give yourself the chance to feel all of your feelings. Brush none aside, and consider none too frivolous or indulgent to experience. Cry if you need to, laugh, stomp around, get angry, even allow yourself a little self-pity. It is important that you let your emotions come up and through you and release them. All feelings have a natural course that they need to run. Blocking them will only block you from moving on.

DEALING WITH CRISIS

Owen had what he believed was a fantastic idea for a new Web site that he was certain would succeed. He had been addicted to the Internet since before it was fashionable, so he understood what that culture was all about; he also was quite adept at business. After reading about all those people whose online e-commerce sites had gone public and had made fortunes, he was convinced his would be successful, also. He left his high-paying job as an investment banker, gathered private investors who gave him sizable amounts to start the company, leased office space, and hired a staff.

With only four weeks until the official launch of his new Web site, Owen and his staff worked around the clock. Living off caffeine and adrenaline, they were all exhausted and irritable yet hopeful that their hard work would pay off. The office was charged with excitement.

When the investment money ran out, Owen used his personal savings, confident that he would reap the return on his investment. When that money ran out, he cashed in a portion of his IRA, again confident that he would not only reap the return on his investment but also earn enough to pay the penalties.

The site launched, and at first, public reaction was enthusiastic. But then the daily hits dropped dramatically. The number of consumers who were paying to use his service was less than a quarter of his projections. Owen and his staff tried everything, including spending even more money to advertise and market the site, but nothing seemed to work.

Within three months Owen's company was leaking too much money to stay afloat. Most of his staff had left, moving on to more promising ventures, and a good portion of his advertisers pulled out. It was clear that Owen had no choice but to declare bankruptcy.

When the last paper was signed and Owen closed the doors to his office for the final time, he was bereft. He had lost not only his business but his life savings, as well. He had disappointed his investors, many of whom were his former colleagues and friends at the bank, and his self-esteem was badly damaged. His dream and confidence lay shattered at his feet like shards of broken glass. He felt like a complete failure and spent the next few weeks mired in a deep depression.

It took several months before Owen was able to recover from the pain of his loss. With the support of his friends and family, he eventually pulled himself out of his depression and started the slow process of starting anew. He realized he had been under the spell of a potential fortune and that what he really wanted to do with his clean slate was go back to his original career as an investment banker. He found a position at a new bank and is once again thriving. He does not regret his attempt at entrepreneurship, as he says he would never have known it was not for him if he had not tried.

The darkness that Owen experienced is called the trampoline effect. The trampoline effect states that the lower you allow yourself to go, the higher you can reach. It is also important to have anchors nearby so that you don't allow yourself to go so low that you can't recover. Again, the paradox is allowing the full experience of nothingness without "believing" that it is irreversible. Like the phoenix rising from the ashes, transformation happens when the essential self emerges out of the remains of the unreal persona.

When life deals you a crisis, it is important to see the opportunity, to seek the value, to see how the perceived tragedy presents you with something unanticipated. People who survive adversity and trauma have what it takes to make great things happen. The real key is that they know how to bounce back and move forward.

Bouncing Back

The test of success is not what you do when you are on top. Success is how high you bounce when you hit bottom. —George S. Patton

Bouncing back is the process through which you grieve your loss, then pull yourself back up and start again. It is one of the major keys to success. Those who are fulfilled are those who never gave up trying to be.

As you are fully processing the physical, psychological, and emotional aspects of a disappointment, you will begin to start to notice that you are still alive. Some people think that they can't possibly endure the setback, that somehow during the process, they will die, because it is all too much for them to bear. Noticing that you are a survivor of the experience is an important awareness. This is called *being in present time*. You are no longer reliving the past over and over again in your mind but are ready to "be" present in the here and now.

The next thing that surfaces is the notion that there might be a future. Considering a future means that you are ready to look in front of you and imagine that you have options. Creativity enters the picture when you believe that you actually could envision a life, map out a plan to make it happen, and then set about moving from one step to another. You consider possibilities that you never imagined before and you begin to set goals, activities that you are once again on the game board of life.

You will need to assess whether it is wisest to continue working toward the same goal you were striving for before or whether it is better to formulate a new one. You also will need to determine a new course of action, one that builds upon the lessons you learned from the setback and that revises your plans as needed.

After a disappointment, your initial goals will not be monumental. They will be tiny incremental baby steps. They won't be steps backward regressing toward the good old days, nor will they be directing you around in circles not quite knowing what to do with yourself; these new steps will be steps forward toward your future. Your new future may even be similar to your past, prior to the setback. You now, however, can approach your future with wider eyes and the benefit of wisdom gained.

Even though they are not giant steps with significant achievements associated with them, your new goals are going in the right direction. Make sure you acknowledge them. Be careful not to discount, discredit, or disqualify them because they are not at the level of your previous accomplishments. Part of moving forward is giving yourself permission to be at a different, albeit new, level of achievement. As the expression goes, sometimes you must "go slow in order to go fast."

It is important that you pause as you rebuild your life and thank those who supported you through the disappointments. Don't overlook them as you regain your confidence and get on with your life. It is also important that you stop to celebrate the fact that you made it through the dark times and are on your way to a new future.

LOOKING FOR THE LESSONS

There is no education like adversity.
— BENJAMIN DISRAELI

The moments of disappointment and the perceived failures in your path are all preparation for the one moment when you overcome all obstacles and realize your goals. These perceived failures are rich and fertile ground for learning valuable life lessons, if you are willing to mine them. These lessons not only shape you as a person, they show you what you needed to learn so that your future efforts will yield more positive results.

It is not easy to see lessons in the middle of a disappointment.

Usually in hindsight you can see why something happened. In the middle of the setback, the most common response is "Why me?"

Not many people ask themselves in the eye of the storm or even once things have settled down entirely, "What am I supposed to learn from this?" Doing this is expecting too much. It is, however, a possibility to ask yourself after the incident, "What did I learn from this disappointment?" "How did I grow from this experience?" "What did I get from this experience that I wouldn't have received elsewhere?" In asking these questions, you position yourself to learn and grow from everything that happens to you in life. No disappointment, setback, trauma, or tragedy becomes so devastating that you cannot glean something of value to take with you to the next experience. Successful people learn from everything that happens to them. They become victorious in situations where others see themselves only as victims.

The question most often asked is: "How do I find the lesson when I feel like a victim of circumstance?" The answer is, you don't. You can't have perspective when you are inside the experience. You must gain some distance before you can see what your lessons might be. So the first step is to let yourself feel the feelings, whatever they may be. Do not force yourself to be "big," enlightened, or superconscious before your time. After you totally feel the feelings, there will be a moment when they actually dissipate. At that point, you can ask yourself what you learned from this experience. You can, as they say, see the light. Most people have the lessons of communication, responsibility, forgiveness, and power. All people have individual lessons that are specific to their lives.

- If you want to start your own business, you will definitely deal with the lessons of courage and trusting yourself.
- If you are married, have children and a career, you will be faced with the lessons of boundaries and balance.
- If you are multitalented and have a tendency to job-hop, your lessons will be choice and commitment.
- If you have had setbacks and disappointments, then your lessons will be healing and faith.
- If you are a type-A perfectionist and drive yourself, you will have the lessons of compassion and patience.
- If you expect success immediately, you will be faced with the lesson of patience.
- If you have been downsized or passed over for a promotion, then you will be faced with the lessons of acceptance and self-esteem.
- If you are a superstar and lean toward arrogance, then you will be given the lessons of humility and surrender.
- If you have been presented with an extraordinary opportunity, then your lessons will be graciousness and gratitude.

Everyone has lessons to learn, regardless of where each person is on the food chain. If you don't learn these lessons, they will surely be repeated in your life until you do.

Which lessons are currently appearing on your game board?

Setbacks occur; that is just a fact of life. What really counts is not the size, scope, or impact of your perceived failures. Whether you have been passed over for a promotion from the mailroom or you lost a million dollars in an IPO, what truly matters in the end is how you perceive the experience, what you learn from it, and what you do about it.

If you dwell on it, you will get stuck. If you learn from it, however, it can be an opportunity to go on to succeed beyond your wildest dreams. In fact, it might even take you where you might have gone if life had provided you with a smooth road to travel. The bumps and obstacles are what make the journey interesting and what sharpen your tools for succeeding in the future.

RULE EIGHT

Managing Your Resources Maximizes Your Efforts

Your time, energy, relationships, and finances are your most valuable assets. Handling them wisely enhances your ability to succeed.

L ife is ephemeral. You are here for a brief moment and then you are gone. Yet while you cannot turn back the clock, you can take control of your life while you are here on Earth by managing the various resources that are within your control.

We all have been given a certain amount of resources. Some are intangible, such as your talents, attributes, skills, and tolerances. Others are tangible, such as time, money, energy, and relationships. The tangible resources have limits, they are perishable; there is an end to their reserves. Use them wisely and all your efforts will be enhanced; squander them and you will need to double your efforts to accomplish half as much.

Time, energy, relationships, and finances are all elements that either enhance success or impede it. The degree to which you can have all four of the elements working for you, rather than against you, will maximize your chances for success.

There is an old story about an impoverished man who found a one-dollar bill. As he looked at it, he thought to himself, "I'm thirsty and cold, I think I'll get myself a cup of coffee." As he was approaching the coffee shop, he thought, "When I buy my coffee, the money will be gone." He thought about all the different things he could do with his dollar bill.

As he was pondering this, he looked down and saw a pencil on the ground. He thought, "If I buy some pencils, I could re-sell them and then have two dollars instead of one." So he went into the stationery store and bought all the pencils he could afford for one dollar. Then he went out into the street and sold each of the 25 pencils for 25 cents each. He then had $6.25. He went back inside the store and bought all the pencils he could purchase for $6.25 and repeated the scenario. As the story continues, the moral is clear: You can either spend your resources or take care to use them discerningly. The wiser you are in choosing how to use your resources, the more effectively they work on your behalf.

Resource management is like the Aikido of life. If you learn how to work with the energy at hand—balance it, arrange it, and work from within it—life will function optimally. You will be, as they say, "in the flow."

ORGANIZATION IS KEY

Organization is a philosophy and a system by which you run your life. It is the blueprint from which you construct the various aspects of your existence: how you live, how you function, what you accomplish, and how you ultimately feel about yourself.

When you are organized, you are able to choreograph your activities, your efforts, and your energy gracefully. You can step back and assess the various components of your life, see what needs tending, and take the necessary steps to align your intentions and your efforts. Things work smoothly, because you are prepared and in control at the helm of your life. You are, in fact, steering your own ship.

Is organization mandatory for success? No.

Does it help? Without a doubt.

Think of it this way: If you wanted to drive from New Jersey to California, the best way to do it probably would be to put fuel in the car, get a map, and have the car engine serviced before you leave home. If you plan your trip in this manner, you can concentrate on the important aspects, like driving safely and taking in the lovely vistas along the way.

Now imagine what your trip would be like if you started out with no gas or map, and the car was in need of engine work. Most likely you would spend some of your time lost, parked on the shoulder of the road flagging down help, or waiting in a mechanic's garage for your spare parts to arrive. All things considered, this is not exactly the ideal road trip.

GETTING IT TOGETHER

I am probably not the first person to tell you that an organized life is something to consider. Most likely you have heard this since you were a child, when one or both of your parents tried to teach you why it was important to clean up your room. Perhaps one of your teachers tried to encourage you to develop good study habits through outlining papers and planning your homework. Many people resist being organized because it seems dreary and uninteresting, lacks spontaneity, or appears too rigid.

Yet within organization lies freedom. It gives you freedom to create, to think clear thoughts, and generally to live life calmly and effectively, as opposed to being weighed down by dangling tasks, half-forgotten ideas, time constraints, and general chaos.

Organization also enables you to project an air of professionalism. It makes you appear to be efficient and in harmony with yourself and your life, which of course has a direct impact on how others perceive you. Harmony is simply more attractive energetically than chaos. When you exude an attitude of calm, you imply reliability, maturity, and mastery.

People frequently ask me how I juggle all the components of my life without going crazy. Between presenting workshops both in the United States and abroad, writing books, giving speeches around the globe, consulting with corporate clients, managing relationships with my staff, raising my daughter, and nurturing my marriage, things can get pretty intense. It was even worse when I was a single parent in graduate school. Given all that, I can appear to be inherently superorganized. However, I certainly wasn't born this way.

When I was younger I was one of the world's worst pro-crastinators. Like so many other people, I needed to reach a breaking point before I realized I needed to do things differently. As a college student, I practiced the classic crash studying method, in which I usually put off preparing for my exams until a few nights beforehand. Then I would stay up late into the night and try to cram a semester's worth of information into my head. Then I would take the exam, retain none of the knowledge, and have little to show for my efforts besides a passing grade and bloodshot eyes.

At a certain point I realized that I was causing myself a tremendous amount of stress and anxiety, not to mention cheating myself out of learning properly. I asked myself if that was really necessary, and of course it wasn't. Why, then, was I doing it? When I came up with no better reason than it was more fun to go out with my friends than stay home and study in advance, I immediately assessed that the pressure, stress, and panic, in the end, outweighed the fun. I decided to change the way I had been doing things, learned better habits from a few friends in the dorm who seemed to be able to balance a social life and schoolwork, and organized my life in such a way that I could make adequate space for both.

At the heart of organization is the balance of time and energy. When those two elements are in smooth working order, the pieces of your life seem to fall into place and synchronize in the same way a clock works.

Organization is not so much about where you put your car keys as it is about the deeper level of the connection between you and the various pieces of your life. When you begin with the basic element of coordinating your time and making conscious choices about how and where you spend your energy, the individual particles of your daily existence begin to fall into place.

Efficiency is not valuable in and of itself. When you imagine saving precious time, eliminating stress, or being able to relax, however, it takes on a whole new meaning. In that light, working efficiently is your best ally and one of the most precious skills you can master.

What you value is reflected in how you allocate your time. If you have many goals, high aspirations, and want to succeed, but also want to live a balanced life, then it helps find ways to make all the puzzle pieces fit together.

MANAGING YOUR TIME

We have time enough if we will but use it aright.

— GOETHE

Who you are is comprised of every second that encapsulates your life from the first breath you take to your final exhalation. This hourglass runs until your time has expired. When your time has run out, the game of life is over. Your life, in the end, is the sum total of how you spent your time.

Many people believe there is a final accounting when the game ends. The accounting tabulates the bottom line of how you lived your life. Were you part of the solution or part of the problem? Did you alleviate challenges or exacerbate them? In the final accounting, possessions, status, and bank balances don't count. All that counts is how you chose to use the time that you were given.

You get precisely the time that has been allotted to you, no more and no less. As the saying goes, "Use it or lose it." Since your life consists of the sum total of choices regarding how you chose to allocate your time, it stands to reason that the level of success you achieve in your life will correlate directly with how wisely you used your time. Using your time well is a skill that is developed with practice.

No one is born a master time manager. Managing time is learned through trial and error and through specific lessons, some painless and some uncomfortable. As you review your life, you may see periods when you used your time well and other chunks when you feel it was wasted. Taking this idea to the extreme, the two polar opposites of time management are compulsively driven and lazy. The more preferable way to approach time management is through choice, balance, and focus.

Where Did the Time Go?

Have you ever found yourself wondering where the time went? Have you ever looked at your watch and marveled that so many hours passed since you were last aware of the time? Have you ever stopped and thought, "Wow—it's almost time to go home," or "The summer is over—it just flew by!" Most people have had this experience at one time or another, since life, after all, is about living and not watching the second hand make its routine sweep around the digits.

In those moments when you lose track of time, is it because

you were so caught up in enjoying yourself that you simply forgot to watch the clock? Or was it because you realized that you got caught short yet again? In other words, do you feel good about the way you spent that time, or do you realize with dismay that it slipped through your fingers once more?

If your answer to the question is because you were thoroughly enjoying yourself, congratulations! That means you are able to be fully engaged in your present reality and celebrate moments that matter. This happened to me when I was on vacation with my family in Australia. We were horseback riding in the bush, admiring the breathtaking mountains and enjoying being in nature sharing this experience together. At the end of the day, when I dismounted, I looked at my watch and was astonished to see that eight hours had flown by! I had been so present in each moment that I completely left the confines of minutes and hours.

If your answer is the latter, however, time management may be an issue for you. If you are one of those people who often races to get places on time, who completes projects late, and who feels pressured and rushed, then time is working against you instead of for you.

Caryn was someone for whom time was a persistent problem rather than an ally. She was consistently late, so much so that her husband, coworkers, and friends came to expect her to show up between ten to thirty minutes late for any meeting. She frequently ate on the run and returned phone calls to people's voice mail late at night because she hadn't found a moment to call them back during the day.

At work, she often found herself rushing around at 5:25 to make the 5:30 FedEx pickup, and she made most deadlines in the final moments. It was not out of character for her to be racing through the halls to get to a meeting. Not surprisingly, Caryn was exhausted most of the time. She remarked that she felt like a whippet dog chasing Whizmo, the make-believe rabbit, around the dog track: running yet never able to catch up with her target.

Does this sound like you? If it does, either you can continue on the track you are on and hope that by some miracle it will eventually come together, or you can choose to learn some new skills that will alter your relationship with time dramatically.

Time is a neutral element. It does not have any particular feelings about anyone or anything; it does not care whether it works for you or against you. Deny its true worth and it can feel like a constant burden of restriction. Allocate it wisely, however, and it can appear to stretch before you like a canvas of limitless possibilities.

The Link to Self-Confidence

At the end of the day, when you crawl into bed and draw the covers up around you, there is a feeling. It is either a sense of accomplishment or a sense of disappointment, fullness or emptiness. Either you rest easy, satisfied with the way you chose to spend your precious moments that day, or you experience the uneasy sensation which suggests you squandered something in a way that was less than ideal.

That feeling is something you can have control over. If you set up your day in advance in order to accomplish all of your tasks, you will feel a deep sense of satisfaction. If your own apologies, reasons, and excuses take you off course, they will cause your day to derail. If you plan what you want to accomplish each day and actually do it, you always will feel like a winner when you lie in bed at night.

The bottom line of time management is this question: Are you strengthening the building blocks of self-confidence, or are you eroding them? The laws of nature dictate that energy is constantly shifting; nothing is static. Every action you take—every second you use—is either life-enhancing or life-diminishing.

What does this have to do with self-confidence?

Everything, because the underlying element here is your self-respect. When you lie in bed feeling like a winner, you feel good about yourself and have some measure of pride in your ability to manage the pieces of your day. Such feelings can be contrasted to those times when you try to sleep, but your mind is whirling as you enumerate all the things you didn't get done, all the items you forgot, and how time simply slipped away from you. In those moments you feel ineffective and less than pleased with your day's efforts. If you string enough ineffective days together, you start losing your clarity and your self-confidence can suffer severely.

Take Jeff, for example. Jeff had big plans ahead of him. He had graduated from art school recently with high grades and strong recommendations. He knew he was talented and planned to create four or five paintings to show to a gallery owner who was interested in his work. Since he worked at home, Jeff kept unstructured hours, which proved to be an unproductive formula for him. He often slept late, did minimal work in the afternoon, and then went to dinner with friends.

Several months passed and Jeff realized that he was behind on the goals he had set. He promised himself that he would be more diligent about his working hours. However, he continued to let himself off the hook, and he was unable to change his habits. At the end of each day he felt dissatisfied about not completing any paintings. As the nights turned into weeks, Jeff was creating excuses in his mind as to why he couldn't possibly have adhered to his schedule. Each night he made a new resolution, using the most famous procrastinating mantra of all time, "Tomorrow I will start my new schedule." The next day was the same story, and so it went.

Without realizing it, Jeff was chipping away at the edges of his self-esteem. By repeatedly breaking his word to himself, he was establishing a pattern of self-distrust. Since the way you feel about yourself in one area is contagious and affects the way you feel about yourself in general, Jeff began to feel less secure about his ability as a painter. He was creating an image of himself. Through not doing what he promised himself, he was subtly manifesting a self-concept that was less than esteeming. That lack of confidence was beginning to affect the rest of his life.

Handling your time well has to do with your relationship with yourself, not ultimately with the expectations of others. No one outside Jeff's studio really minded whether he stuck to his self-initiated schedule or not. The only person who was affected by the discrepancies between word and actions was Jeff. Jeff's belief in his own word was at risk. If you can't rely on yourself, what else is there? As Janis Joplin advised, "Don't compromise yourself; you are all you've got."

Can you trust yourself to do what you say you will do? Can

you count on your commitment to make the result happen within the time frame that you have set?

If the answer is "yes," then you have the time management chip. If the answer is "no," you may need to learn some new skills, change some habits, and take some steps to get back to a state of self-enhancement.

LEARNING THE TOOLS

In order to get a grip on your relationship with time, you can do several simple exercises. These exercises will heighten your awareness and help you make choices that will, in turn, help you manage your time in a way that is productive, effective, and life-enhancing.

The time log

The first exercise is called a time log. This exercise is ideal for people who often get to the end of their days and have no idea where the time went. If you frequently find that you are busy but that the results you ultimately produce are less than what you had hoped, try this exercise for one week and see what it brings up.

The time log requires a pad of paper and a pen on the side of your workstation or carried with you as you go through your day. At the end of each hour, log how you spent your time. For instance, 9:00–9:30 organized paperwork, 9:30–10:00 made follow-up calls, 10:00–10:15 sent faxes, 10:15 met with George, and so on. If you are more comfortable, you can log the information on to a document on your computer. Do this exercise for one week. At the end of the week, take your job description, or the overall goal that you were trying to do that week, and place it next to your time log. Then ask yourself the following questions:

1. In light of my job (or goal), was each task in alignment with what I am here to do?
2. Could any portion of my time have been better spent?
3. Did I waste any time or effort?
4. If I could redo this week, what would I change?
5. What changes do I want to implement next week?

The main benefit of this exercise is to discover how much time you actually spend on tasks, as opposed to how much time you think you do. As is the case when many people sit down to create a money budget, you might be surprised to discover how much time you actually are spending on certain activities. This exercise allows you to honestly assess where your time is allocated, so that your awareness level is heightened. When you are aware and have acknowledged the actual truth of the situation, you are then able to make changes.

The perfect schedule

This second exercise is called the perfect schedule. This exercise is similar to the first, in that you are heightening your awareness about where your time goes and precisely how long each task takes. In addition, it takes you to the next level, envisioning your perfect schedule and comparing it to the one that you are currently living so you can assess the discrepancies and make the needed adjustments.

This exercise is ideal for people who can't seem to fit all the things they need into their days or their lives. It is less job-oriented and more life-oriented than the time log. If you are someone who frequently feels guilty for not attending to one area of your life, such as your family or your physical health, or you feel that important moments are passing you by, this is the exercise for you.

In order to do this exercise, you will need a blank week. You can take one from your day planner or print one from your computer, or you can always draw one with a ruler and a pen. It should look like a schedule with seven days on it, starting in the morning and ending in the evening, and it should have no appointments or tasks written in yet. On a separate sheet of paper, write down all the tasks, projects, classes, and appointments that you have and that you want to include in your ideal week. Include all work-related responsibilities, family time, exercise time, sports, hobbies, volunteer work, and time alone (if that is an option). Complete your list to your satisfaction.

When it is complete, assign each area to a time slot in your perfect schedule. Begin by first writing in the absolutes: those responsibilities or activities to which a certain number of hours are already accounted. These are the nonnegotiable, fixed allotments of time that already exist in your life. For example, if you know you need eight hours of sleep to function properly, write that in. If you know you need to work eight hours in order to satisfy your job description or get done what you need to, write it in. If an hour of exercise every morning is essential to your physical and emotional well-being, include it. If you already know you have your daughter's soccer game every Saturday afternoon for the three next months, include that. Do not scrimp on any of these fixed time allotments, because you will only be cheating yourself.

Then assess how many of the twenty-four daily hours are left each day after you include the fixed allotments. Into those hours, write in your ideal vision of how you would spend them. In other words, fill in the "variable" list of activities in the spaces in between the fixed ones. Would you spend them with your spouse? Working on a hobby? Reading? Whatever else was on that original list of activities that you want to include in your life, find a space for them on your perfect schedule.

After you have done this, you will find one of two options: Either everything fits perfectly, or there isn't enough time in your life to do everything you need and want to get done. When you have completed the final piecing together of your perfect schedule, look at it closely and ask yourself how you feel. The answer could be "great!" Or the answer might be "exhausted," or "there is no time for me!" If the latter is the case, then you will need to rethink your original choices or reconsider your allocations and do some juggling. Now for the second part of the exercise.

Draw, print, or take another blank weekly schedule, and put it alongside the original perfect schedule that you already filled in. As you go through the motions of living your life, log into your new schedule how you actually spend your time. At the end of the week compare the perfect schedule with the actual schedule and notice any discrepancies. If the two match up perfectly, congratulations!

If there are discrepancies, however, one of several things

might have happened. First, you might discover that the original choices you made about your fixed time allocations do not fit your definition of an ideal life. You may find that you want to alter the fixed time blocks. Perhaps you will discover that you resent having to spend the number of hours you do at your job or that you do not want to give up one day each week for tennis lessons. If this is the case, you have less of a time management issue to deal with and more of a life-path choice to address. If this is the case, go back to Rule Three and carefully listen in to what is right for you.

For example, Albert was a manager in a healthcare consulting firm in Sweden. He loved his job and the people who worked with him. He was in charge of all the resources for the firm, including videos, books, periodicals, and all Internet capabilities. After reviewing the results of Albert's tests, I commented that it must be very difficult for him to be isolated and apart from people all day, as his test results showed he was an extreme extrovert. His response was "I don't mind." I was quizzical and probed him further. "You see, at ten-fifteen I go for coffee with some colleagues; then at twelve I go for lunch with others; at three o'clock I go for coffee again with others; and at five o'clock some others join me for drinks." I asked him how he got his work done, and he told me that was precisely his problem because there was no time. He had to get all of his work done in the evening, because the day hours were already taken up. This was causing him a lot of stress because there wasn't much time for sleep and he was tired all the time. Albert would have been better suited to a marketing job where he would have been paid to meet and talk with people all day long. As the media resource, he was at cross-purposes with himself; to get his needs met, he threatened his job.

Another thing that might create discrepancies is allocating too much of your time to pleasing others rather than yourself. Listen closely to your explanations to yourself of why you did not do all the things you wanted to. See if the justification sounds as if other people are in control of your time. Listen to hear if saying "no" is something you need to learn. Maybe having clearer boundaries would help. Perhaps you need to practice being forthright with people who are time gobblers. Consider putting your tasks and projects first and helping others when yours are complete.

Graham was what most people would call a workaholic. He was excellent at his job, loyal, accountable, dedicated, and tops in his field. The only problem was that his personal life was suffering. He loved his wife and children, that wasn't the problem, nor was he inefficient. His biggest problem was that he was overly accommodating. Conversations that could have taken five minutes stretched out into twenty. People stopped by his office to say "Hello," and he didn't have the heart to say that he was racing against a deadline and didn't have time at that moment. He was polite and gracious to a fault. His Southern hospitality acted against him when he found himself at the office late at night finishing up the work that didn't get completed during the day.

With lack of sleep, no time to exercise, and minimal time with his wife and children, the whole world started to converge on Graham. When he came to my Inner Negotiation Workshop, he was dumbfounded when he discovered that one of his greatest assets was also one of his biggest liabilities: giving generously of his time. Graham resolved to make some changes, no matter how uncomfortable they might be. Clarifying the purpose of meetings, being more conscious of office drop-ins and miscellaneous time gobblers, and being willing to say "no" were the key behavior changes he needed to implement. Obviously Graham didn't transform overnight; he required some practice to change his behaviors. Eventually, however, he integrated his new set of behaviors into his modus operandi. Little by little he created boundaries, and conditions in his life are now within his control.

Ask yourself what aspect of your life you want to change. With a little thought, most likely you will be able to assess which parts of your perfect schedule you are willing to change your actual life to accommodate.

Once you have done this, you will need to take pen to paper and map out your game plan for how you will rearrange your schedule. It might be difficult, but you may need to bump some things that are taking up too many precious minutes. Move the pieces around until you can make it all fit. Remember, there are only twenty-four hours—no more and no less—so be realistic and discerning about how you plan to spend your precious time.

The pie chart

Another exercise for time management is the pie chart comparison. It is the same as the perfect schedule exercise, except that it utilizes percentages rather than linear pie charts.

I find this method is better for people who can wrap their mind around numbers more easily than words. The exercise works like this: Take two sheets of paper. Draw as large a circle as will fit on each sheet. Then take a third sheet of paper and list all of the responsibilities, projects, tasks, and priorities that you spend your time doing. This list could include generic categories, such as work, family, social activities, cultural experiences, church involvement, educational time, community service, sports, exercise, and time with self. Include every category that occupies your time.

After you have completed this list, assign percentages next to each item. The percentages should equal 100 percent, no more and no less. Then take one of your circles and carve up the pie according to your percentages. This pie chart is your current reality. Then take the same list, draw a vertical line down the page, and assign new percentages to the categories, the ideal allocation of your time. Then take the second circle and carve up the pie with your second set of percentages. This second pie chart represents your ideal time allocations at this stage of your life.

Juxtapose the two pie charts and ask yourself what would need to happen for your current reality to shift toward your ideal picture. The purpose of this exercise is to see the discrepancy between the two and to map out a plan to shift your percentages from how things are to how you want them to be.

All three exercises—the time log, the perfect schedule, and the pie chart—are designed to achieve the same outcome: to become aware of your current time habits, acknowledge what you would like to do differently, and give yourself the opportunity to choose to do things differently. When you make the needed adjustments that these exercises reveal, you will know what it feels like to lie in bed at the end of the day knowing your day was well spent to your highest good.

CULTIVATING YOUR RELATIONSHIPS

The more he gives to others, the more he possesses of his own.

— LAO-TZU

Into the tapestry of who you are is woven every relationship that touches your life. These relationships are the fibers of your connections to the human network around you.

Each relationship in your life is an investment of your time, your energy, and you. Each one of these extensions has an invisible tentacle that is connected to you. Relationships can either be problematic or solution based; they can infuse you with energy or drain you; they can either enrich your experience or deplete it. Basically, the manner in which you interact with each person in your life will impact your overall well-being.

Whether the person is your boss, colleague, peer, subordinate, client, customer, or even part of your personal support network, if the person relates to you, he or she takes up a certain degree of your consciousness. Whether the relationship is functional or dysfunctional, temporary or permanent is up to you. You must stay current with what is happening between the two of you; it is important that you tell your truth and stay aware of how the relationship affects your life. You will contribute to those whose lives you touch and be enhanced by those with whom you have contact.

The people in your life can be your greatest resource. From them you can gain support, glean wisdom, and learn valuable lessons. You can come to understand the true meaning of reciprocity and hone your skills of listening, supporting, managing, and serving. Whether positive or negative, each relationship offers you a wealth of knowledge as well as numerous opportunities to grow.

BOSSES AND MENTORS

From your superiors you can gain wisdom and understanding. Either they can serve as a model for how you want to function, if you find them admirable mentors, or they can serve as silent warnings to you of how *not* to function, if you find their actions and behaviors unproductive or unsavory. Particularly difficult bosses sometimes can provide the best lessons.

For example, Pam worked as a publicist for an executive in the fashion industry who was known to be demanding and difficult. Her boss, Walter, was a brilliant visionary, and with that came unpredictable behavior, extreme moodiness, and frequent unreasonable expectations. One moment he would be commending Pam for her good work on one project, and the next he would storm into her office and chastise her, "We're behind the eight ball. Why weren't you on top of this?"

There is a theory that having a difficult boss is one of the best training experiences there is, and in Pam's case, this was certainly true. From this particular relationship, Pam learned several valuable lessons that would contribute to her future success. First, she learned how to be ultra-responsive and think on her feet, which is always a good skill to develop. Second, she developed patience and tolerance, by learning to deal with larger-than-life people whose egos frequently took over. Third, and perhaps most important, she witnessed behaviors that she vowed she would never repeat when she was in a position of authority in the future.

Ruth, on the other hand, had a totally opposite experience. Ruth worked for Lorna, the vice president of communications for a conglomerate. Lorna manages a team of highly qualified and talented professionals. She is bright, talented, task-oriented, and interested in the happiness and well-being of her team. She often calls departmental meetings to assess where everyone is in terms of progress and stress levels, and encourages her employees to ask for what they need in order to get the job done. She pays attention to the personal details, such as births, marriages, and deaths, and of course the professional benchmarks, such as promotions and company anniversaries. She recognizes her staff members for particular achievements, thanks them regularly for their good work, addresses tough issues when appropriate, and presents criticism in a way that is constructive. As a result, her staff feels her positive energy, and, as Ruth put it, most would "walk through hot coals for her."

From watching Lorna, Ruth learned how to produce excellent work while exhibiting interpersonal skills. She often asked Lorna for her advice on difficult assignments and listened to any criticism from her with open ears. She used

Lorna as a role model, and from her she learned the importance of treating people with dignity and respect.

Not every boss is a mentor, nor is every one an evil entity portrayed in the "Dilbert" comic strip or on some TV sitcoms. Most are somewhere in between. It is always to your highest advantage to develop a relationship with your boss that not only advances your career but enhances your life skills, as well.

COWORKERS

Your coworkers or colleagues are like your work siblings. Assuming that you are peers, there will be times when you are in direct competition as well as times when you must pull together for the common good of all. Relationships with coworkers are among the most important to cultivate, since your colleagues are the ones you will need to rely on, trust, and work in harmony with in order to succeed.

If you have colleagues, that means you work in a company setting. If you work in a company setting, that means you must deal with some element of politics. The secret to navigating your way through the political maze is by maintaining your integrity, doing your job with excellence, and formulating healthy relationships with those around you.

Do you support your coworkers? Do you cheer them on, celebrate their successes, and acknowledge their accomplishments? Do you willingly lend a hand when they need it and express empathy when things don't go as planned?

Or do you view your colleagues as stepping-stones? Do you practice unfair competition? Are you a regular at the water cooler, ready and eager to spread unfortunate news or pass along gossip?

Arnie started in the mail room. He was ambitious, focused, and determined. He spent his free time learning about computers, he chose his mentors wisely, and he didn't waste a minute. As he climbed the corporate ladder, he learned how to be resourceful. He made great strides, with annual promotions and raises. His success was strategic and meteoric. Yet there was one thing missing: Arnie lacked an attitude of gratitude.

Arnie saw his opportunities and seized them. When people were no longer useful to him, they were off his radar screen. At first people within the company saw him as motivated; over time that perception started to shift into viewing him as a master manipulator.

The greater his power and prestige in the organization, the more fierce became his opportunism. He thought little of screaming at someone to the point of breakdown, of sending his assistant out to do personal errands for him, of telling his subordinates that they were not worth their salaries. There were even some individuals who had to enter therapy after working closely with him. People wondered whether he had a chemical imbalance or whether he was unstable, but those who had known him over time knew that achieving his objectives was his total preoccupation. People were pawns in his game, to be used for whatever they could contribute and then discarded.

As it turned out, Arnie was caught in the crossfire of a corporate merger; when the music stopped, he was without a chair. On the street, without a job, Arnie tried to revive his old contacts with his former colleagues. The memory of how he had treated them lingered over time, and now it was Arnie who was having trouble getting past the gatekeeper. Arnie discovered the old and familiar truth to ambition: It is important to remember that you see the same people on the way down as you did on the way up.

When it comes to colleagues, remember the golden rule. They can be great assets to you or stumbling blocks, depending on how you treat them.

CLIENTS AND CUSTOMERS

Clients and customers are the bread and butter of any business. They need to be treated and maintained as valuable resources, for without them, all you have is a product or service with no one to use it.

When it comes to service industries, the human element is equally as important as the sale. Everyone has an experience of the salesman who is your best friend before the sale is made and then doesn't recognize you after your credit card has been run through. Those behaviors are easily detected, and word travels fast. If you want to be known for your ethics and authenticity, you must focus on giving your customers and clients what they want, not what you have to sell.

Listening is essential if you are to discover what they want. Focusing on clients' wishes, on their needs, on their concerns is what separates salespeople from those committed to service. It is the outstanding salesperson who will be honest and tell you when a product is not right for you. Even if the salesperson doesn't close the sale that day, you will never forget the person's integrity. That memory will linger, and you will return for another dose of truth that probably will result in a sizable sale some day.

Many excellent books teach more about interacting with clients and customers. Since it is such a broad topic, I will simply pass along a wise and wonderful quote by Mahatma Gandhi that I think summarizes the essence of client and customer service.

I never thought that Gandhi was a proponent of customer service, but when my sister was in India, she visited his house and found this quote of his. I personally think the world would be a better place if each of us, regardless of profession, would embody these principles:

> *A customer is the most important visitor on our premises. He is not dependent on us. We are dependent on him. He is not an interruption of our work, he is the purpose of it. He is not an outsider to our business, he is a part of it. We are not doing him a favor by serving him. He is doing us a favor by giving us an opportunity to do so.* — MAHATMA GANDHI

WAYS TO NURTURE BUSINESS RELATIONSHIPS

Human beings are social creatures. However, most of us require some coaching in order to interact effectively with the people in our business life. Here are eight important ways you can tend to these relationships so that both you and they can succeed to your highest aspirations.

I. **Always keep your word.** It has been said that you are only as good as your word. Keeping your promises and doing what you say you will do is how you earn the trust of others. If you are known as reliable, you will attract more business, earn the respect of those who work with you, and polish your reputation to a rich sheen. You also will feel good about yourself and therefore will be naturally inclined to do better in the world. Doing what you say you will do lets others know that you are someone to be counted on and reinforces your self-respect.

2. **Appreciate those around you, and let them know it.** Be sure to thank them for work well done, for their support or guidance, or for their business. Thank them in both words and actions. A verbal "thank you" is a great basis, yet every now and then there needs to be more. Pay attention to how you feel when thanking them, and also to their reaction. If the verbal recognition does not feel sufficient, you will know. Then decide what is needed; perhaps a public acknowledgment, flowers, a raise, or a bonus will let them know how you feel. Do not take anyone for granted. Honor everyone's contributions and acknowledge the part they all play in your work life.

3. **Go the extra mile for them.** If you do this even though it does not benefit you directly or immediately, you will embody "right action." Doing this will not only create goodwill and make you feel good about yourself, it also will serve as a personal deposit in the karma bank. Remember, what goes around comes around.

4. **Treat others with respect.** Listen when they speak. Show up on time. Be responsive and timely with phone calls, faxes, and e-mails. Pay attention to their priorities, not just your own. Treat them as people worthy of consideration.

5. **Forgive when necessary.** Forgive mistakes, practice empathy and compassion. As long as people put forth their best effort and conduct themselves honorably, make room for the occasional error.

6. **Honor the human in them.** Show your coworkers that you care about their well-being. Be interested and involved with their victories and disappointments. My mother always took the time to inquire about the families of people who supported our family. The carpenter, the policeman down the street, the cleaning lady were all treated with respect, concern, and genuine interest. As a result, all would strive to go the extra mile for her in exchange.

   Within each person, regardless of his or her title or job description, dwells every facet of being human. If people feel valued by you, as a person, they will become a precious resource, not merely temporary coworkers.

7. **Pay attention to the details.** Make it easy for people to do business with you. Take the obstacles out of their way. Make their day brighter by easing the stumbling blocks. Listen to their needs and wants. Do what companies like Amazon.com do and pay attention to what

your customers buy. Then make recommendations based on that information. Build loyalty and trust, which in turn increases your business.

8. **Communicate clearly.** Articulate your expectations. Express your concern when necessary. Ask for what you need.

Most people are not mind readers. Be clear about your intentions, your desires, and your needs. Ask for the same in return. It will save time and effort if you get this information right the first time.

MAINTAINING ENERGY

Living in balance and purity is the highest good for you and the earth.

—DEEPAK CHOPRA

Through each one of us flows a life force. This life force is our connection to the greater universal source of energy that affects all living creatures. The potency of this life force in you fluctuates in direct proportion to how much you expend versus how much care you take to recharge it.

Energy is the fuel of life. It is difficult to see or hear, but you can undeniably feel its presence or absence. We all require energy to be successful. It is essential for mental acuity, physical endurance, and emotional stability. Without energy it is impossible to pursue your goals and to succeed. How you generate it and use it and how often you recharge it has a direct impact on your ability to succeed.

STAYING IN BALANCE

You have heard the cliché about what work and no play can do to a person. Beyond making people dull, however, it also can have a negative impact on their physical, emotional, and spiritual well-being, not to mention on their ability to be productive.

There is such a thing as pushing yourself too hard. It's one thing to work hard and give 100 percent; it's another to repeatedly ask the universe to lend you an extra 15 percent beyond the reserve that you have been given. From time to time you can overdraw your energy account, but if you do it too often or do not repay the loan, eventually you will bounce your efforts.

Overexertion is more than just physical exhaustion, although that is a large part of it. It is emotional drain, when you give more than you have without taking the time to replenish. It is spiritual deprivation, when you neglect to feed your soul. There is an overall sense of apathy, a lack of motivation, which inevitably leads to feelings of "What is this all for?" When you push yourself beyond what is reasonable, you can easily lose sight of your purpose.

Thomas was an Episcopalian minister with a congregation of 250 parishioners. On a weekly basis, he gave sermons, visited sick congregants in the hospital, performed memorial services, and worked with the board to manage the business of the church. He was always on call, since spiritual crises and acts of God knew no time boundaries.

Often Thomas's wife, Penny, would try to convince him to take some time off to refuel. She watched Thomas give spiritual guidance and keep himself on a restricted regime of work interrupted by brief intervals of sleep. As the months went by, Thomas began to look drawn and fatigued, and he became irritable with her and their two children. Eventually, migraines convinced Thomas that even ministers need to care of themselves if they are to be of service to themselves, others, and the universe as a whole.

How can you tell if you are off balance? It's really quite easy. If you wake up just as tired as when you went to sleep, if you feel sluggish throughout the day or get sick frequently, then it is a sign that you need to take better care of yourself physically. If you feel weighed down, pressured beyond what is normal for you, or have little motivation, your emotional battery might be drained. If you start wondering why you are doing any of this at all, your spiritual reserve needs replenishing. If you start imagining throwing everything away and heading for a deserted island, that's a clue that you are long overdue for a vacation.

Pay attention to these signals. They are telling you what you need.

SPENDING ENERGY WISELY

Everything you do requires energy. Every action you take, every thought you have, every emotion you feel demands an expense of this precious resource. If you monitor how much energy you spend on what, you can begin to make choices on where you want to allocate your energy.

Energy doesn't stand still or stay in one place; it shifts. Where it goes and how it goes is up to you. To be in charge of your energy, you must know what works for you. You need to be aware of those elements that energize you and those items that deplete you and choose between them as necessary.

It is draining to spend time in places and circumstances that do not authentically resonate for you. How do you feel when you come home from an event you "had to" attend versus one that you were excited about? My guess would be less than energized.

Similarly, it can be tiring to spend time with people who do not vibrate at compatible frequencies with you. Those who talk only of themselves or those who are overly demanding of your attention can make an afternoon with them feel like an eternity.

This is not to say that you always can choose to do things that you like and be around people that make you feel good. In a perfect world this is so, but in reality there will be times when you need to come into contact with energy drains. The key is to keep these experiences to a minimum, so you can save your precious energy for those things that make you feel most alive.

Sometimes energy can be depleted unwittingly. Worrying about someone or some event can diminish your supply. Whether you know it or not, your lingering to-do list of incomplete projects, unresolved choices, or unreconciled issues requires energy. These issues occupy parts of your consciousness and require attention. If you do not purge yourself of thoughts, they cling like wet leaves to the edges of your consciousness. They continue to occupy the foreground of your mind and eclipse other concerns.

Not long ago, I was writing and I had a tight deadline; I

also was preparing to go on a business trip and organizing my daughter Jennifer to go to college, all at the same time. While none of these was particularly draining in and of itself, holding them all in my mind was exhausting.

Unexpressed or unprocessed emotions are another slow energy leak. Those things that you do not attend to linger in your awareness, lurking in the shadows and silently pulling on your reserves. Unexpressed anger, disappointment, and loss all weigh you down. They keep you from being in the present moment. If you sense that this is the case, it will come as more of a relief than anything else to acknowledge the unexpressed emotion, deal with it, and release it from your energy field.

This is where techniques like journaling and list making are useful. These tools are effective ways to get thoughts on paper; this way energy is conserved that otherwise would be wasted trying to remember all that you must do. In addition, meditation is an excellent way to clear your mind of lingering thoughts, feelings, and to dos that might be draining. If the thoughts and ideas are truly important, write them down. If they are not, release them to the universe and move on.

When it comes to spending your energy, the bottom line is to view your vitality as a valuable resource and make choices according to your priorities. If you waste it on cluttered thoughts, unprocessed feelings, and people who take more than they give, there will be no energy left for those things that will fulfill you and bring you happiness.

RECHARGING

Without energy, your vehicle will falter. You may sputter along, but you certainly won't zip around the track. Energy, like time, is a valuable and limited resource. The difference between energy and time is that energy can be regained. You can always get more energy, if you go back and recharge.

Frequently I hear people say that they simply don't have the time or the opportunity to recharge their batteries. There is too much to do, too many calls to make, too much to read, too many pages to write, too many numbers to crunch, to find the chance to revitalize. However, recharging is not a luxury; it is a necessity. How can you expect to run on empty for very long? How far will that take you?

Exercise, sleep, and nutritious food are nature's universal rejuvenators. Beyond that, however, each person is unique and recharges in his or her own way. It is up to you to determine how to reenergize your mind, body, and spirit.

How do you recharge, rejuvenate, and restore your energy? Is it through reading novels, relaxing with your significant other, practicing yoga, playing with your dog or cat? Do you feel invigorated by a magnificent sunset, the scent of lavender or vanilla, or the taste of pralines and ice cream? Do you feel peaceful when you are meditating, riding your bicycle, or working in your garden? Be sensitive to environments that restore and rejuvenate and others that drain you.

Build at least one energizer in your life each day. Check in with yourself, pay attention to the signals that indicate that you are running on low and due for a recharge. The signs may feel like fatigue, or stress, or take the form of a headache or a general lack of motivation. Notice these cues and clues. Most of all, take care of yourself. You want to make sure you are healthy enough to enjoy the fulfilling and successful life that you are creating.

If you find yourself slipping back into the I-don't-have-time-to-recharge excuse, remind yourself that you are all you've got. After all, if you don't restore your vital reserves, who will?

MANAGING YOUR FINANCES

When you start really respecting yourself, those you love, and your money, the result is that you start having control over your money. What follows from that is control over your life. — SUZE ORMAN

Finances are similar to time. Whether you are aware of it or unconscious about it, money goes. It goes somewhere, and the two ultimate questions are: Do you know where your money goes? Are you in control of how your money is spent? There are no "right" answers to these two questions. There are only choices and consequences.

Maggie, the daughter of a friend of mine, had her first summer job as a lifeguard at a local summer camp. Over three months, she earned $1,600, yet at the end of the summer, she had nothing to show for her hard work. When her mother asked her where the money went, her answer was "I don't know." Upon thinking about the question, she enumerated, "I spent the money on coffee, drinks, food, movies, CDs, makeup, shoes, and some presents for friends." Her mother asked if it ever occurred to her to save some for the future. She replied, "No."

After this conversation, it became clear to my friend that some discussion on money management was in order. Not that it was necessarily wrong for Maggie to spend her money on entertainment or fashion, but she might be establishing an unconscious life pattern of earning and spending that was not the most prudent in the long run. First and foremost was the awareness of where the money was going.

Maggie and her mother had a discussion about money as a resource. Her mother said that money was like energy, here and gone. If you didn't know how to conserve it, you could wake up one day and find out that you didn't have any left. She also suggested that money could be divided into three piles: a now pile, a later pile, and much, much later pile. The now pile was for immediate, simple pleasures: coffee, movies, gas, and CDs. Later was for sometime in the future, three months to one year, for larger purchases: rent, food, clothing, car expenses, trips, and the like. And the much, much later fund should go into savings for school and should be touched only in case of emergency. Maggie was quite interested to learn this concept. Previously she had considered money only as a form of instant gratification. If you have it, you spend it. She had never really done any long-term planning; conserving and saving were new concepts.

Some people are adult versions of Maggie. They are used to spending every cent they earn. If they earn more, they spend more, and so on. It is important to look at the big picture and choose what you want to achieve with your finances, both in the short term and in the long term. If you never learned it from your family, your teachers, or your role models, learning to save is a skill that must be developed. Saving and investing in the right vehicles also helps accomplish objectives that you might wish to fund in the future.

Managing your finances creates peace of mind. Life costs money, and knowing how much you have and consciously choosing where and how to spend it puts you in the driver's seat. It allows you to live gracefully as opposed to clutched with fear, anxiety, or panic about insufficiency and survival. When you are at ease, your life—and hence your ability to succeed further—just flows better.

Consider taking a course, listening to a tape, joining an investment group, subscribing to a magazine, buying some books, or meeting with a financial advisor to further your knowledge about financial matters. If you can understand what your unconscious beliefs and decisions are regarding your relationship to finances, then you can become aware, acknowledge what you discover, and make the choice to change your behaviors.

Successful people, by and large, have come to terms with their resources and have made conscious choices about each area. So too must you assign values to your time, people, energy, and finances. The more aware you are, the more effective are your choices.

Resources are limited; they are to be used at your discretion. If you are mindful of those variables that are within your control, you can make wise choices about the allocation and use of those resources. How well you manage them will determine how far your efforts take you.

Ultimately, either you manage your resources or they manage you.

Which shall it be?

RULE NINE

Every Level of Success Brings New Challenges

Each accomplishment alters your reality, either slightly or dramatically. Your task is to maintain your balance when your game board shifts.

As you pursue the realization of your goals, exert the required effort, and manage your resources wisely, there is a good chance that you will attain at least some of the results you are seeking. Crossing the finish line, however, is not the end of the game. In fact, it is really only the beginning of a new set of challenges and life lessons. When success enters the picture, a new reality is created and the game board shifts. The challenge presented to you is to keep your balance as you rearrange the pieces of your life to make space for your new reality.

Newton's third law of motion states that for every action, there is an equal and opposite reaction. If you follow this logic, it makes sense that any success you achieve will cause ripple effects. These ripple effects can include changes like identity revisions, increased responsibility, and dealing with different reactions from those around you. Dealing with such changes is the unexpected fine print at the bottom of every dream realized and every new level of success attained.

George Bernard Shaw once said, "There are two tragedies in life. One is to lose your heart's desire. The other is to gain it." While succeeding at your goals may not necessarily cause pain akin to heartbreak, it certainly comes with its fair share of rewards and challenges. You will need to make your way through the happy rewards, the new responsibilities, and the surprising and unfamiliar landscape that success brings.

THE HERE VERSUS THERE MYTH

Rule Six in *If Life is a Game, These are the Rules* states that "There" is no better than "here." As I explained in that book, wherever you are is your current "here." When you strive to get to "there"—someplace beyond your "here"—you may buy into the myth that "there" is superior to "here." Yet in reality, "there" is no better than "here." It is simply different.

Every "there" shimmers on the horizon like a pot of gold. It may look like the solution to all your problems, the panacea for whatever ails you, or the utopian version of your current life. In reality, however, even that pot of gold, miracle cure, or utopian fantasy doesn't come without its own set of challenges and lessons.

Moving from "Here" to "There"

Change happens. Situations change, people change, and success happens. When you succeed, however, everything doesn't suddenly become all better. The myth is that when you finally achieve the success you have been yearning for, everything will be perfect. As humans, we transform as old lessons are learned, new levels of success emerge, and new challenges surface. We don't shed our issues entirely; we simply trade them in for new ones that may look and feel quite different.

Success merely changes the game. Old concerns, such as monetary restrictions, cramped living or work space, freedom concerns, doubts, fears, or insecurities, may vanish. New concerns then appear and present challenges that in your previous circumstance you might never have imagined. You may suddenly have to deal with increased stress, new rules and expectations, and the overwhelming pressure of stepping into a life that is bigger than the one you knew.

When the Internet company Gloria worked for went public in a big way, her shares suddenly became worth a tremendous amount of money. She believed that all of her problems would be wiped away instantaneously now that she really didn't have to worry about money. She was right that the old problems, such as paying her rent on time, buying shoes and clothing for her three children, and having to cope with getting around on public transportation in the rain, would vanish. What she hadn't counted on were the new challenges that came with her newfound financial security.

Suddenly, as it is wont to happen when large sums of money are involved, relatives she barely knew showed up on her doorstep with their hands out. Her ex-husband, whom she hadn't heard from in six years, reappeared on the scene. She started receiving so many solicitations for credit cards, life insurance, and charitable donations from every registered non-profit organization that her mailbox was overflowing daily.

Internally she was struggling, as well. Making choices about how much to spend on what preoccupied her thoughts. Having cash available was a new concept for her, and she felt uncertain about it. She had never been very savvy with money, and now she was forced to learn how to balance her checkbook and work within a budget rather than just struggling to make ends meet. Most of the time she was fearful that she was doing the wrong thing or that people would dislike her because she wasn't generous enough.

While the pot at the end of Gloria's rainbow was certainly making her life easier on one hand, it also was causing her some uncomfortable growing pains. Unlike other people to whom success or riches do not come overnight, she needed to stretch herself to fit her new reality very quickly. Sometimes, late at night, when she was by herself, she found herself a bit wistful about when her life was simpler. But then she would look out the window at her shiny new Mustang convertible and laugh and shake her head. Were the adjustments uncomfortable? Of course they were. Would she trade it all and go back to the way things were? Probably not.

"This" begets "that"

A wise yogi once said "When you get this, so you get that," and he could not be more accurate. Every "this" comes with a "that." The "that" is not necessarily negative or burdensome, but it always carries equal weight to the "this."

For example: If fame is your goal, you will need to contend with the idea of a public life. Most Olympic medals come with body aches and physical exhaustion. Great wealth comes with the demand for advanced financial systems, and promotions usually go hand in hand with additional responsibilities and added pressure. Marriage means learning to give and take, and entrepreneurship is accompanied by risk.

I am in no way suggesting that all good things come with a negative underbelly. What I am referring to is the unbreakable link between choice and consequence. The universe operates with a stimulus/response reaction. If you act and stimulate a situation, there will be a response—positive or negative—either in the same circumstance or in another one.

DEALING WITH THE CHANGES

All change is a miracle to contemplate.

—HENRY DAVID THOREAU

Success can be a wonderful thing. There is nothing quite like the feeling of realizing your goals and seeing your dreams come true. It can make you feel on top of the world and aligned with your purpose. You may experience unbridled bouts of joy and intense pride, or you simply may experience a deep sense of satisfaction and fulfillment.

As we have seen, however, with success come details to be addressed and changes to which you must adjust. Some changes will be positive, some may be challenging, some may be fun, and some may be tedious. Regardless of how you feel about them, these changes require your attention to ensure that your newfound success is not undermined by your own hands or by the reactions of others.

PREPARING IN ADVANCE

In order to deal with the changes, it helps to have anticipated changes in advance. Knowing what you can expect before you step up to the next level is the best way to make your transition as seamless as possible.

Being fully informed about the whole picture that you are about to step in to will help you deal with the reality of the situation. When you are aware in advance of the joys and trials that the realization of your goal will bring, you can prepare yourself with the necessary tools. The less you are caught by surprise, the more stable the new ground will feel under your feet. You cannot, of course, anticipate everything that is to come, but it certainly helps to have a good idea of the basics.

For example, Scott and his wife, Bari, were both therapists who conducted seminars for couples. They were relatively well known in their community but not known nationally. That is, until they were asked to appear on a national talk show. After they appeared on the talk show, their business tripled, and they were hard-pressed to keep up with the demand for their services.

Being overloaded, however, was not really the problem. The problem was that they were both stretched to the maximum and started taking their stress out on each other. They spent so much time counseling other people on how to have healthy relationships that their own union was suffering from neglect.

Scott and Bari were caught by surprise. They had not

known that such success would be so taxing on their relationship. Furthermore, they had no systems or agreements in place to manage the strain. Thankfully, they both had well-developed communication skills and were able to get themselves back on track, but not without some scrambling. The transition probably would have been much smoother if they had had some idea of what they were headed for.

Asking questions of those who have been where you are going can illuminate what you will need to prepare for the journey. Most people are very willing to share the knowledge gained from their experiences. Ask all the questions, especially the ones you perceive as the dumb ones, because they will fill in the gaps in your vision. Ask about their story, how they felt, what happened, what took them by surprise, what they would do differently. Ask if they had it to do over again, would they? This is one way to avoid the rose-colored glasses that the "here-there" syndrome creates and to prepare yourself for what is to come when you realize your goals.

INTERNAL CHANGES: A SHIFT IN IDENTITY

Two components make up what we call our "identity." The first component includes the roles we play in life: the actions we take, the choices we make, and the way we conduct ourselves in the grand scheme of things. External trappings include roles like mother, father, assistant, employee, woman, dog owner, nurse, coupon-clipper, football fan. Externals also include how others see you, such as a promising musician, person with limited funds, and hopeful entrepreneur. All of these expressions and defining aspects of who you are compose part of your identity.

The second component is the relationship you have with yourself. This is comprised of how you perceive, regard, and feel about yourself. This part is the more important of the two and is also the one that you will need to attend to when the external factors shift in new directions.

Each time you expand to a new level of success, your identity is slightly altered. This can happen in increments, with annual raises, or it can happen all at once, when your company is taken public, your team wins the national championships, your invention is patented and sold, you win the Nobel Prize, or you break the land speed record. Regardless of the type of success you achieve, when your status, sphere of influence, or bank balance changes significantly, your identity also changes. Who you were and how you defined yourself have been altered. You are no longer the person who lived from hand to mouth; you are no longer average or normal; you are no longer a "nobody"; you are no longer the person who looks up at others in awe.

You are no longer a promising musician; you are now a musician with a record contract. You are no longer a person with limited funds; you are someone who operates from a place of sufficiency. You are no longer an assistant; you're a manager. You are no longer a hopeful entrepreneur; you are a flying success. You have become what you desired; you have fulfilled a part of your dreams. As a result, you know intuitively that something in the interpersonal fiber of your identity has changed.

Frequently, we hear of a Hollywood celebrity who has had a breakthrough in his or her career, and the next thing the newspapers report is that the person's relationship or marriage is breaking up. There are, of course, many possible reasons why relationships fall apart; however, success, when not handled well, can shake up if not destroy the infrastructure of your life.

How do you deal with changes in your identity? How do you process alterations in who you are? These are important questions. There aren't easy, pat, standard answers. The process is a little like growing into a larger pair of shoes. They may seem awkward and uncomfortable at first; you may think, "This is not me," and for the most part you are right. It's not who you were, it is, however, who you are becoming.

"Becoming" is by definition a transition. It is the emergence of a new you. It is establishing new ground and new anchors and finding comfort with what is inherently uncomfortable. This happens in gradual stages.

For eight years I worked long and hard to complete my master's and earn my doctorate. When I finally graduated, I wasn't sure how to act. I wondered if I should introduce myself differently or sign my name differently or act like a Ph.D. (whatever that meant). I felt uncomfortable because I had accomplished something I had dreamed about for over twenty years, and yet I still seemed like the same person. I still got up in the morning, had my cup of tea, and put on my pants one leg at a time. So, I asked myself, "What's the big deal?" I wanted the world to know that I had achieved something that was, in fact, a big deal for me, but I didn't want to brag.

I thought the solution was to have a party and to send out announcements. I had new business cards made with "Ph.D." on them. I also transformed the guest room into my official office with my degrees on the wall. These steps still weren't enough for me actually to "get it."

Finally it became clear that I needed to do some inner work. I had to integrate the various parts of me: who I was, what I had achieved, and who I had become. This was like psychic microsurgery, but I will explain the process.

I made three lists:

The first list was *how I defined myself in the past*:
Management consultant
Single mother
Student striving for a degree
Capable public speaker
Talented trainer
Able person in search of credibility
Invisible supporter and empowerer

The second list was *what I had achieved*:
A breakthrough
The highest level of education achieved by anyone in my entire family
A new belief in my own abilities (I can, I did it!)
I conducted original research
I discovered that I loved being a student
I felt my brain expand with new knowledge and information
I experienced a new level of expertise and authority

The third list was *who I had become*:
A doctor of philosophy
The highest level of achievement in my field
A recognized authority

A person with more self-respect
A professional who could now teach at a university
A person who feels secure about herself

By making these lists I identified, acknowledged, and artic-
ulated the transition that I was wrestling with. Externalizing
my internal transition helped me integrate the experience.
Whenever you can ritualize, process, or externalize what is
happening in your life in order to integrate yourself with your
development, you establish your new reality. Becoming is the
process of merging the external with the internal.

Acknowledging your success

Each level of success is a rite of passage. If you don't acknowledge it in some way, you could easily gloss it over or take it in
stride. You don't have to write out the transitions, as I did (although I certainly recommend this exercise), but you need to
experience the reality that something has changed and to become fully cognizant of what that change means to you.

Talking to a friend or your mate could be helpful. The
most important part is addressing the feelings that you have
about yourself. How are they different? What has changed
about your relationship with yourself? What will you do differently? What do you need to anticipate or plan for in the future? All of these questions will bring up a degree of discomfort. That is normal. You may feel a desire to regress back to
an earlier state, a time when you were more comfortable with
your situation or your status. If this is true, notice it. Ask
yourself what it will take for you to fully embrace your new
level of success and do whatever you need to do.

Ritualizing your success

Ritualizing the attainment of your success is the final piece of the puzzle. Mark your success in some way, whether it is hanging your diploma, celebrating with your nearest and dearest friends, or going out and buying yourself a new watch. Choose something that will symbolize your success each time you look at it or recall it, so that it can serve as a reminder of your achievement.

We ritualize other important events in our lives, such as the union between couples and the birth of children, so why not individual accomplishments? Doing so will create an indelible memory that will linger long after you have moved on to the next big thing.

EXTERNAL CHANGES: THE REACTIONS OF OTHERS

While you are, of course, an individual with distinct physical and emotional boundaries, you do not exist in a vacuum. You are part of the larger human chain that links you to everyone around you. What happens to you affects them, whether directly or indirectly, in major ways or in minor ones.

The concentric circles around you of your core group, your inner circle, your friends, your associates and colleagues, and your acquaintances all create your sphere of influence. Since you are at the hub of this wheel, you must reintegrate in a whole new way into the world in which you were previously. You must sort out how you present yourself and address any reactions that come your way.

Success tends to bring out the best or the worst in people, including those around you. When you experience a win in your life, a sifting process always occurs. Your true friends will step up to the plate in your moments of glory. Those who cannot, however, may fall to the wayside. It is painful but true that as you expand, you may outgrow some relationships, or vice versa. That contingency presents challenges.

There are those who will be genuinely excited about your promotion, your raise, your graduation, or the new opportunity you have been presented with. These are your true supporters, the mature associates, and the family members who can see beyond their own needs and celebrate with you your endeavors. These relationships are precious and should be acknowledged for all they offer you.

Frequently, however, you will discover that there is at least one person who is envious of your success. This person may be threatened by your achievement and appear less than supportive of your new good fortune. Perhaps the person feels excluded or deems the recent rewards undeserved or unfair. Whatever the reason for the person's negative reactions, being on the receiving end can be confusing and hurtful.

For example, Susan and Russell were cousins who always had shared a close relationship, since they were the same age and had similar interests. They were both seniors in college and at schools fifty miles apart, and they frequently helped each other out by trading notebooks from classes they had taken in previous semesters. They often interacted as friends outside of the normal family gatherings. Susan often turned to Russell for advice about men and dating, and Russell liked to bring Susan shopping with him because she had excellent taste. Everything was harmonious between them until Russell discovered he was selected as valedictorian of his graduating class.

Susan did little to hide her jealousy, although it showed up in the guise of casual disdain. She started calling Russell "the brain" and made offhand snide comments about his grades. On Russell's graduation day, Susan arrived late and left his celebration party early, claiming she had a headache.

Although she tried to appear flip in front of Russell and the rest of their extended family, inside she was housing a volcano of emotions. On one hand, she was proud of her cousin, but on the other hand, she was extraordinarily jealous. Although she graduated with decent grades, she certainly did not receive any honors. She begrudged Russell all the attention he received. While she felt some shame about her reaction, she could not seem to help herself.

When I met with Susan, it was clear that Russell's success had struck a nerve in her. With a little questioning, we uncovered feelings of intellectual inadequacy that Susan harbored and identified them as the reason for the behavior she was displaying.

As is often the case, when people around you cannot rise to the occasion and be happy for your success, usually some feelings of insecurity about themselves are at the root of the behavior. Whether they are aware of it or not, your success shines a bright spotlight on what they perceive to be their own flaws and shortcomings. Their jealousy or resentment could very well be the seed of an unfulfilled dream.

In these situations, your natural reaction might be to feel hurt and even angry. From there, however, you can do one of two things: You can banish this person from your life, either physically or emotionally, or you can search for a way to remedy the situation.

Sometimes the only thing to do is to say a gentle good-bye to the relationships in your life that do nothing but pull you down. They can have diminishing effects. If you have experienced this scenario, you know there are two options: Have a frank conversation with the people telling them how you feel and what you want, or let them fade gracefully from your life.

However, if your heart tells you this is a relationship worth fighting for, then a different approach is in order. First, stop and ask yourself if there is anything in your behavior that might be causing a negative or nonsupportive reaction in the person. Are you gloating, lording your newfound success over the person, or simply ignoring him or her? Is there anything that you have done that might have alienated the person? Be honest! If the answer is yes, you will need to take responsibility for that and make amends.

Next, try to put yourself in the person's shoes. What could he or she be feeling in light of what has changed for you? Perhaps the person feels scared that he or she might lose you, or concerned that he or she won't measure up to your standards anymore. Often women who become engaged overlook the fact that the news might be alienating to their single friends with whom they previously spent every Saturday night; men who make the company softball team forget that their buddy who didn't make the cut might feel rejected. People who get promoted frequently miss the cues of resentment from those who were previously their peers.

Find a way in which you feel comfortable to address the subject. Determine an appropriate time and place and be empathetic and compassionate. You will need to address your perception of the situation and listen to what your friend is saying without judging or interrupting. Hear the person, feel what he or she feels, and resist the urge to "fix" the situation. Ask if there is something that your friend desires, perhaps a discarded dream that he or she secretly would yearn to pursue and haven't. Ask what you can do to support the person and explain what you want both for and from him or her.

If friends resist your efforts, refusing to own up to the situation or unwilling to discuss their feelings, all you can do is let them be. I once met a woman named Rochelle who arranged flowers. Rochelle had learned everything she knew from an older woman who was her mentor. When Rochelle started her own business, her mentor was jealous and fearful that Rochelle would steal her clients. Thus often she tried to undermine her protégée's business. Rochelle tried to address the situation with her, but her efforts at communication were brushed aside as "nonsense."

I asked Rochelle how it was that she appeared so calm about this hurtful situation, and she replied as follows: "I can't get myself tangled up in her negative web. What I can do, though, is pray for her, hold her in the light, and send positive thoughts her way. That's what gives me peace about the situation."

You may need to do as Rochelle did, and find your peace with the situation any way you can. In the end, you always will know that you tried your best.

KEEPING PERSPECTIVE

We are well advised to keep on nodding terms with the people we used to be, whether we find them attractive or not. We forget all too soon the things we thought we could never forget. —JOAN DIDION

One of the biggest challenges to succeeding is maintaining your perspective. Before you reached your new level of success, you were familiar with the view. You knew the landscape and were well acquainted with the terrain. It all looked reassuringly the same every morning when you awoke.

Then the game board shifted, and nothing looks familiar anymore. The view changed, and the terrain may feel foreign under your feet. Everything seems different.

It is easy to get swept up in the excitement and seduced by the glamour and thrill of the victory. The true test of what you are made of comes when you realize the goals you have been striving toward all along.

Can you enjoy your success without letting it distort your vision?

Can you embrace your new level of success without it inflating your ego?

Can you stay aligned with your values when new temptations beckon?

The greater your success, the more challenging the tests. At a certain level of playing the success game, you will likely encounter four significant lessons: maintaining integrity, arrogance, greed, and power. The more you achieve, the harder it is to resist seduction by the dark side of success. Your greatest challenge will be to stay grounded in yourself as you scale the heights of greatness.

MAINTAINING INTEGRITY

Integrity means doing the right thing, especially when no one is watching. It is easy to act honorably when others are present to give credit for your actions. It might be convenient, however, to take the easy road or deviate from honor when no one is present. The true test is how you behave when your actions are witnessed by you and you alone.

The word "integrity" comes from the root "integer," which means "whole." To live with integrity means that you align and encompass all aspects of your being into your actions. You live from a set of personal values that dictate your behavior. These values permeate everything you do; hence your life is lived holistically and authentically.

Maintaining integrity is one of the highest lessons to learn in terms of human evolution. It is a lesson that often comes up when you succeed, for it is then that you may be called upon to compromise your values in order to proceed. Integrity demands that you remember who you are in light of your success and honor that person.

What do you stand for? What principles do you embody? Do you have the moral fiber to stick with them when no one else is looking or when compromising your values looks like it might accelerate your speed or progress?

We live in a society that sorely lacks integrity. Whom do you know who wouldn't exceed the speed limit if it was the middle of the night, on a straight road with no other cars around? Would anyone you know find a suitcase of money on the side of the road and take it to the police?

Doing the right thing takes fortitude. It requires tuning in to your conscience, listening to what it says, and honoring the values you know to be correct. Many times as you travel along on your journey you will be faced with situations that demand that you choose between your conscience and getting ahead. That's just the nature of the game.

Bella, for example, was a young actress from Italy I knew years ago when I was still acting. She had come to America to study acting. She loved the theater and grabbed on to every opportunity to excel in her art. She had studied Shakespeare, the classics, and George Bernard Shaw. One day, after auditioning for a new director, she was taken aback by his offer for a "private audition." Since she was new to the nuances of the English language, she did not understand what he meant and innocently asked him to explain.

"Come back to my place later," he encouraged her, "and you can audition for me privately." Now the message was clear.

Bella considered her career goals side by side with her values. She desperately wanted the part in this director's play, as it would be a tremendous boost to her career. On the other hand, who would she be if she accepted a part based on something other than her acting ability? In this one moment, Bella's naïveté about the world vanished, and she knew that this wasn't the last time she would face such a choice.

"That's all right," she answered. "I think I'll pass. Thanks anyway." As she walked away, she breathed a sigh of relief and didn't look back.

Sometimes the choices we are presented are less black-and-white than Bella's. Sometimes it is a boss asking us to do something that makes us feel uneasy, such as stretching the truth. Or it might be the temptation to take a shortcut that looks foolproof to reach your goal. These moments are hard, because we observe situations daily that reinforce that in today's world we must compromise ourselves in order to succeed.

You will know if integrity is one of your life lessons if people or situations repeatedly try to seduce you to compromise your values. In these moments you may feel conflicted or in crisis. If you stand for some principles, if you know your values, you must ask yourself if the cost is worth the choice to ignore or abandon them. The conflict can be as large as stealing from your company or as small as cheating on an exam or taking the credit for someone else's work. Almost always it will seem as if departing from your values and principles will bring a quick and large payoff.

What can you do in these moments? You have to weigh the consequences of your actions, consider the payoff, and make a choice. These questions might help in your assessment process:

1. What do I stand for?
2. How will I feel if I do or do not take this action? Is the payoff worth the feeling?
3. Is this action in line with how I define myself?

4. Will this choice get me where I want to go? Or is it a detour?
5. If I do this, will I feel proud of myself?
6. What are my alternatives?
7. What are the possible consequences of doing or not doing this?

THE TRAP OF ARROGANCE

The greater your success, the more challenging the tests. As you evolve in the levels of your life, you will realize that you have learned many lessons well. So well, in fact, that you may have passed all the tests you have been given. As you look back and see the lessons in your past, you may have the tendency to believe that you have "arrived" and thus have no more to learn. This is the most seductive lesson of all, for it is beyond pride; it is arrogance.

Arrogance occurs in people who have achieved something and believe that they independently caused their own success with no assistance, support, or input from others. Arrogance presumes that you are invincible, above everyone else, and beyond reproach. You assume that the rules apply to others but not to you. You feel as if you have earned the right to behave any way you want without adverse consequences. Arrogance is having an attitude of superiority, delighting in your own significance and thriving on other people's feelings of inferiority.

There is a fine line between pride and arrogance. That line is called ego. It is perfectly normal to take pride in your accomplishments; those are a direct reward of your efforts. The danger zone is when you start thinking that your accomplishments earn you the right to be condescending, obnoxious, or even abusive. The paradox is being confident while eschewing conceit and believing in your self-worth without overestimating it.

People sometimes feel seduced by arrogance. The perception may be "Now that I am 'someone,' I can treat others any way I want." If you have been diminished in your past, then you might be tempted to belittle others. If you have suffered in the past, consciously or unconsciously you might want to see others suffer, as well. The expression "power corrupts absolutely" basically says that when some people experience power, they are seduced to abuse it rather than use it effectively and ethically.

Gavin, for example, fell into the trap of arrogance when he got his big break in broadcasting. He had been delivering the weather on a local station in Wyoming until a station in a major city chose him out of the thousands of others to be their anchorperson. Gavin was ecstatic, and wasted no time in letting everyone around him know he was "on his way to being a star."

Gavin arrived at his new job puffed up and rather impressed with himself. He ordered around the interns as if they were servants, overlooking small details like "please" and "thank you." When one of them brought him coffee with cream instead of black, he wordlessly handed it back to the young woman with a disgusted expression. He interrupted his colleagues regularly and even called one of the most respected anchorwomen in the country "hun." In short, he behaved less than graciously all around.

I know this story because the executive who hired him is a friend of mine. As she told me the story, ending it with an exasperated "can you *believe* this guy?" I told her that I could. I had certainly seen it before. I suggested to her that she just wait it out, because sooner or later the universe usually provides lessons of humility to those who need it the most.

Humility is the best cure for arrogance. Unfortunately, often we don't see our own foibles. When we don't, the universe gives us a dose of humiliation rather than a self-selected ounce of humility.

Have you fallen into the trap?

If you have become arrogant, most likely you are unaware of it. No one usually admits—or even knows—that he or she is arrogant. How can you tell if you have fallen into the trap? Well, if you view your subordinates as underlings, or people who deserve less respect than you, or if you tend to forget your personal evolution by which you attained your success, then it sounds as if you have. Perhaps you believe that you have learned all the lessons that you are here to learn or think you already know all that you need to know. You might believe that your success is permanent, that it cannot be taken away from you.

If any of this sounds familiar to you, some degree of arrogance has you in its steely jaws. The only way for you to break free without having to wait for the universe to do it for you in a way that can be painful is to return to an attitude of gratitude. You need to remind yourself that all greatness comes from a source that is larger than you; you are the vessel through which it is expressed. Maintain your connection to your spiritual source and your higher purpose, and you can pull yourself out of the trap before it is too late.

Greed: The Seduction of "More"

How much money is sufficient? How many awards, accolades, corporate coups, standing ovations, or gold medals are enough? When is your cup finally full?

Marlon Brando once said, "It's the hardest thing in the world to accept a little success and leave it that way." In some ways, success is like a drug. Its effects can be intoxicating, leaving you wanting more, and more, and more. Yet at what point does desire turn to greed and pursuit of dreams transform into gluttony?

The turning point comes when the desire to accumulate becomes an obsession, when you continue to fill your basket, yet it always feels empty, when "enough" becomes a concept that is foreign and distant as the moon.

Greed is a lesson that appears when you begin to scale great heights, especially in the arena of business and money. There is always a grander house down the street, a shinier car to be purchased, the next big deal to close, a bigger venue to fill. When you view these events as goals, you are still pursuing a healthy journey toward new levels of success. When you view these as must-haves, however, you have taken a turn into the deep woods of greed. If your drive has turned into compulsion, the lesson of greed has arrived.

The source of greed

If you are greedy, the belief of scarcity is deeply embedded in your consciousness. The addiction to accumulation comes from needing to fill the hole in your life and ultimately deep in your soul.

Conversely, when you come from an attitude of abundance,

you do not need to grasp on to more, and more, and more, because you inherently believe that there is enough for everyone to go around. You don't worry about getting your fair share because you trust that it will be provided. You have no limits, no lack, no holding back. You view life as if all things are possible, and the universe is a provider you can rely on.

Marvin's life was full of love, satisfaction, quality people, and an abundance of material possessions. From the outside it appeared that Marvin was a successful adult who had everything he wanted—a lovely wife, wonderful children, a beautiful home, fulfilling work, and a network of friends. However, if you listened to him talk, life sounded full of struggle and effort. While talking to his wife about his lack of satisfaction, he admitted his fear. His fear was that every blessing bestowed upon him would suddenly disappear.

Marvin had grown up in a large, middle-class family wondering if there would be enough for him, including food on the table. Although Marvin's circumstances had changed, his beliefs about scarcity and abundance had not. His childhood beliefs were still solidly in place. Even though his life was now full, deep inside he still carried the fear that there wouldn't be enough for him.

Marvin's fear extended into the areas of love, pleasure, and money. He could never seem to get enough of any of them, because he was always nervous that the reserve would run out. The fear robbed him of his joy. He had to make a dramatic shift from "scarcity orientation" to "abundance orientation."

Marvin discovered that F.E.A.R. stands for False Expectations Appearing Real. He quickly checked his present reality juxtaposed with his past fears and realized that the fear was a carryover from his past and not relevant in the present. His conscious choice to open his heart and allow the abundance of the universe to fill his consciousness shifted his reality.

If you sense that you need to make a shift from scarcity mentality into abundance, perhaps to avoid learning the painful lessons that greed can bring, you can begin with simple rewiring of your thought patterns. Identify the beliefs you currently have about scarcity and abundance; this will bring to light any unconscious patterns that may be controlling your behavior. Then use whatever method works best for you—mantras, affirmations, coaching, reading books about abundance—to enable you to imprint new and positive beliefs in your consciousness.

When you know in your heart that there is enough out there for you and that the universe supports you, greed will dissipate and you can relax into the joy of appreciating all that you have.

HANDLING POWER RESPONSIBLY

Power is the ability to manifest your desires in the world. In its purest intended form, it radiates from the source of all life through every human being. How powerful you are depends on how much you trust and cultivate your connection to that source.

To the outside world, especially the world in which we now live, power has taken on a different meaning. It has come to connote the extent to which you have control and dominance over others and the level of influence you possess.

The lesson presented to those who rise to positions of power is one of the most challenging ones there is. There is always a lure toward abusing your power for further personal gain and satisfaction versus using it for the good of all.

Many people promise themselves that once they rise to a position of power, they will not become like the others they have known who abused it. Yet all too often when they reach the levels to which they have been striving, it becomes easier and more appealing to relish their power and use it purely for personal gain.

Perhaps you know someone who has become obsessed with power. Maybe you have crossed paths with one who abuses authority or position. When people abuse their power, they can lose their center and eclipse their purpose.

If you have yet to learn the lesson of power, you will be tempted to misuse it, and tests will be presented. If you don't learn the lesson, you risk becoming disconnected from your values and your principles. Your essential self can become lost in the ultimate pursuit of unbridled power.

Success is not the answer to all your problems. It is not the magic ticket to the kingdom of happiness, nor is it the final resting place in terms of your evolution. Every level of success comes with its own set of challenges that you will encounter and lessons that you will need to learn.

As you continue your journey from your present "here" to the next "there," keep in mind that "there," in the end, is no better or worse than "here." It is merely another opportunity to explore new territory and learn what each new place has to offer.

RULE TEN

Success Is a Process That Never Ends

Each plateau has a new ascent. Once you reach the
top, there is yet a new peak to embrace.

uccess is not a finite state. There is no magic door
labeled DESTINATION: SUCCESS that you enter and
permanently remain on the other side. Success is like
a spiral staircase that you ascend; it turns, bends, and curves
its way through the different plateaus of your dreams.

There are always new heights to reach, new vistas to explore, and new lessons to learn. As you have discovered already, when you reach the elusive "there," another "there"
magically appears, and you become aware of the next level of
fulfillment. Part of the process is determining if you want to

continue to grow, if you can maintain your authenticity while evolving, and if you can keep things in perspective as the game changes. Success is about mastering the balance between appreciating where you are while simultaneously keeping your eyes focused on the next challenge or opportunity that will reveal your continuing personal evolution. It is indeed a paradox that involves holding two seemingly opposite realities simultaneously, which is not easy, but rather a graduate course in the school of life.

THE CYCLE OF ACHIEVEMENT AND RENEWAL

What the caterpillar calls the end of the world, the master calls a butterfly.
— RICHARD BACH

I always have loved climbing mountains. It isn't so much the physical exertion that I value but rather the incredible vistas that you experience each time you put forth the effort to struggle against gravity and reach new heights. My friend Ciska and I were in Switzerland on Le Dent du Midi, a mountain in the Alps. I wrestled with my inner journey of ableness while I hiked and climbed thousands of feet higher onto the snow-covered mountain. As I stretched physically, I noticed myself expanding in new ways internally, especially as we traversed very steep and sheer areas. Each time I tackled the boulder or face in front of me and climbed to the top of the immediate obstacle, the vista opened and the panorama before me revealed even bigger peaks and challenges ahead. It seemed like an unending series of plateaus, valleys, and mountaintops.

Success is similar. As soon as you reach one level, you have a new vantage point that enables you to see a whole new world full of opportunities and challenges that previously were hidden from your view. You might be inspired to reach for higher peaks in areas where you experience success, or you may turn your attention to another facet of your life in which you have unrealized goals. There is always another turn you can take that will enrich your life and bring you an even deeper dimension of fulfillment.

If you have success with your career goals, you may be drawn to turn your attention to your personal ones. As you pursue the creature comforts that bring you joy, yet another opening may appear in the area of health or healing. As you pursue that goal, career opportunities may be launched into high gear as new ambitions surface. In other words, your life is an endless and varied series of mountains to climb, plateaus to enjoy, and new heights to scale. When you have reached each summit, the process begins again in a new area, at a new level, with a new challenge.

The reason why success is a process that never ends is because our definitions of success are constantly changing and evolving. As toddlers, success is the ability to cross the room on your own two legs. As children, merely walking is no longer enough to define success for us. It becomes about reaching four feet tall, or getting our parents to say "yes" to ice cream, or getting As on our report cards. When we grow into teens, success means carving out our individual identities. Then our definition of success may evolve again when we are in our twenties, as it becomes about finding and doing well in our careers, meeting a spouse, or perhaps starting a family. What success means to you will continue to shift as you go through the stages of your life, and each new success you attain expands you in new and astonishing ways. As the author Gloria Steinem wisely said, "To me, the model of success is not linear. Success is completing the full circle of yourself."

APPRECIATING THE VIEW

All this can feel as if you are running on a treadmill if you get caught up in the momentum. Do not forget to stop and notice where you are and appreciate the experience. As is the case with most things in life, however, the pivotal element that dictates whether you feel exhausted by the infinite possibilities or exhilarated by them is your perspective.

All too often, as we slide up and down the chutes and ladders of success, we can forget to pause when we reach a new height to notice, acknowledge and celebrate our accomplishment, and observe the scenery surrounding us. Yet it is those precise moments that we initially strove for. If you overlook the importance and value of those destinations that originally attracted you and rush past them en route to your next adventure, you run the risk of missing the rewards of all your efforts.

Satisfaction depends on where you focus your attention. If you live fully in the present, you will have many more opportunities to enjoy the journey. If you only look to tomorrow, focusing only on the future, you will ignore the moment and may fall into the trap of dwelling on what you don't have rather than on what you do. The key to success is to ride the line between happiness and contentment and to balance satisfaction with aspiration.

For example, Charlie was a social worker who had trouble acknowledging his accomplishments. He was intensely dedicated to helping those around him who were less fortunate or who suffered in some way. He worked in a clinic in Chicago that brought in hundreds of clients each day, and Charlie gave everything he had to help as many people as possible.

Charlie provided financial counseling to families whose primary earner had just lost his job. He found a doctor who could make a house call to a sick baby. He contacted the son of an elderly man with Alzheimer's to ask if he would be willing to take his father into his home. With each person he helped, he never paused to experience the gratification that giving to another would provide him. He always focused on the maximum number of people he could help. This was wonderful in that he helped so many people in need; however, he never took the time to acknowledge and celebrate the positive impact he had on every life he touched. Despite all that he did for so many, Charlie never felt really fulfilled, because he never allowed himself to experience his intrinsic value.

The most severe outcome of not appreciating what you have is stress and, ultimately, burnout. You lose sight of your purpose if you never pause to experience the joy. You could wake up one day with realized goals without the memory of the journey.

RECOGNIZING YOUR ACCOMPLISHMENTS

You may not always recognize when it is time to pause and celebrate your achievements. Life has a way of keeping you so busy that you may be preoccupied and distracted with tasks. It is a good idea to check in with yourself every so often.

Stop every once in a while and ask yourself these questions:

1. What have I accomplished recently that I am proud of?
2. What have I learned from the journey between "there" and "here"?
3. How have I grown?

Asking these questions will put you in "pause" mode. Answering them will give you insight into where you are on your path. By acknowledging and listing those things that you have accomplished and learned, you have tangible proof of your progress. Noticing all the things you have done can inspire pride, and from there you can stop and celebrate your achievements and your growth.

Jill, one of my clients, takes this exercise one step further. She does the exercise not only for herself but also for her company. She and her two partners sit down every December and make a list of all the things they accomplished, from small victories to significant advancements. They write down all that they have learned collectively as an organization, including how and when they collaborated well and what did and did not work on the whole. As a result, they end the year feeling proud of their accomplishments and in command of their future strategy. They also benefit from comparing each year's list to the previous one, charting their growth and development and gaining a perspective on what may come in the future.

Whenever you have the opportunity, stop and appreciate the view from each juncture. Take stock of the beauty, the gifts, and the breakthroughs of the life you are living. Notice as well the promise of the life you are in the process of creating. The panoramic view can be invaluable to your perspective and your self-esteem. While it is always important to stay focused on the goals before you, it is equally important to look behind you from time to time to see how far you have come.

THE MEANING OF THE GAME

What we call the beginning is often the end. And to make an end is to make a beginning. The end is where we start from. —T. S. ELIOT

Success is having lived a life worth living. Yet the grand irony is that the ultimate value in playing the game is not the realization of your goals; rather it lies in truly learning the lessons you are here to learn while playing the game.

When you formulate a goal, you automatically establish the curriculum for your own personal development. You imagine your objective is to achieve your goal. Whether you are conscious of it or not, the journey en route to your destination is where true learning happens, not in the achievement of the objective. Growing is what the game is all about. The lessons you encounter along the way are what enrich you as a person and cause you to expand beyond what you were when you began.

Growth is a process that never ends. By definition, when a

living being ceases to grow, it stagnates and dies. Your experience of being human will encompass many different phases of growth, and each level of success will lead you to the next one.

Everyone has the capacity to improve. No matter how much you have learned, there is always more to know. No matter how accomplished you are, you can always expand. No matter how wise you become, there are always new dimensions of higher consciousness. Those who derive the most from their lives are those who embrace the possibilities and continually strive for more growth opportunities.

In the end, fulfillment is a state of being. It is a feeling deep in your bones that you are happy and that all is authentic and satisfying in your world. Growth, however, is a state of doing. When you are playing the game, you are in action. When you reach the end of one phase of the game, you experience fulfillment . . . and then the process begins all over again.

For as long as you are on this Earth, there will always be new adventures to take, new mountains to climb, and new experiences to learn from. Your time here is all about growing into yourself. The goals you set and the successes you achieve are all means by which you do so. What matters along the way is that you pause every now and then to take stock of what you have accomplished and who you are before you set off on your next exciting journey.

The name of the game is success, and winning is all in the experience.

ABOUT THE AUTHOR

Dr. Chérie Carter-Scott is a *New York Times* No. 1 bestselling author, an entrepreneur, international lecturer, management consultant, corporate and personal motivation coach, minister, and pilot.

In 1974 Dr. Carter-Scott founded the MMS (Motivation Management Services) Institute, Inc., which specializes in personal growth training programs and workshops, corporate consulting, and customized training programs worldwide. For the past twenty-five years she and her partner and sister, Lynn Stewart, have empowered thousands of individuals to redesign their lives personally and professionally. By way of their unique and inspired work, they continue to assist others in initiating life-changing choices.

The Inner Negotiation Workshop is the heart of MMS. This workshop is a human greenhouse in which your authentic self emerges and is given the opportunity to grow. When you are connected to your authentic self, you will be able to envision, articulate, magnetize, and manifest the success you have always dreamed of.

To learn more, you may contact:

- The MMS Institute: 1-800-321-6342; or
  in California: 805-563-0789
- The MMS Institute Website: *www.TheMMS.com*
- If Success is a Game Website: *www.ifsuccessisagame.com*
- E-mail: *cherie@ifsuccessisagame.com*

Other titles by Dr. Chérie Carter-Scott, Ph.D.:

If Life is a Game, These are the Rules: Ten Rules for Being Human
*If Love is a Game, These are the Rules: Ten Rules for Finding Love
and Creating Long-Lasting Authentic Relationships*
*Negaholics: How to Overcome Negativity and Turn Your Life
Around*

Dr. Carter-Scott lives with her husband and daughter in Nevada and enjoys piloting between her Nevada and Santa Barbara offices.

Dear Reader

You possess an inner wisdom—your spiritual DNA—that is always with you to direct you on your path. Your main challenge is to listen, to trust, and to honor what you hear. Success can be elusive until you internalize this concept and make it your own.

Success is in the eye of the beholder; it is defined in your terms. It is as varied as the people who strive for it.

Imagine that you have succeeded if you have fulfilled your potential; you have succeeded if you have been true to yourself; you have succeeded if you have truly loved another; you have succeeded if you have fulfilled your purpose; you have succeeded if you have made your dreams come true; you have succeeded if you have improved your quality of life; you have succeeded if you have made a difference; you have succeeded if you can look back on your life knowing that you have done your best.

If you honor your inner messages, you are automatically a success. Being true to yourself and aligning with your true path are ultimately what separates those who are temporarily gratified from those who are truly fulfilled.

If Success is a Game, These are the Rules has been written for you. It presents the ten rules for a fulfilling life, the universal principles that guide successful people. It is to be used as your companion as you travel the road of life in search of your purpose and the fulfillment of your mission. Use it as a reference book as you pass through each phase. Refer to it when you have questions or if you are confused, uncertain, or fearful that you have strayed from your true path.

If the principles in this book resonate with you, and you want more morsels of universal wisdom, you are invited to continue your spiritual development through our workshops, training programs, personalized coaching, and my other books.

I wish you the fulfillment of all your dreams and success in everything you do.

Chérie Carter-Scott, Ph.D.